What Did Jesus Say About That?

Stanley C. Baldwin

Read this book on your own, or study and discuss it in a group. A leader's guide with hints and helps for a group study based on this book is available from your local bookstore or from Victor Books at $1.95, including visual aids (Victor Multi-use Transparency Masters).

VICTOR BOOKS

a division of SP Publications, Inc.
WHEATON. ILLINOIS 60187

Most New Testament quotations are from *The New International Version: New Testament,* © 1973, The New York Bible Society International. Used by permission. Old Testament quotations are from the King James Version (KJV), as are a few New Testament quotations.

The words of Jesus are in boldface type throughout. Example: He said, **"According to your faith will it be done to you."**

Second printing, 1975

Library of Congress Catalog Card Number: 74-28510
ISBN O-88207-718-X

VICTOR BOOKS
A division of SP Publications, Inc.
P.O. Box 1825 ■ Wheaton, Ill. 60187

To Prairie Bible Institute,
where I learned to dig into
God's Word and to search out
its truths for myself.

About the Author

Stanley C. Baldwin was born in Bend, Oregon, and has lived most of his life in that scenic state. He was founding pastor of Calvary Community Church near Albany, and later served churches in Corvallis and Burns.

He began writing for publication in 1963, his first article being published by *Eternity magazine.* In 1970 he became managing editor of *Power Life* and subsequently executive editor of *FreeWay* and *Power For Living,* publications of Scripture Press. When the Victor Books division was launched in 1971, he became its first editor. Currently Mr. Baldwin lives in Milwaukie, Oregon, where he is engaged in free-lance writing.

Previous books by Stan Baldwin include *Games Satan Plays, Tough Questions Boys Ask* and *Tough Questions Girls Ask* (with his wife, Marge), and *The Kink and I—a Psychiatrist's Guide to Untwisted Living* (with Dr. James D. Mallory, Jr.).

Stan and Marge have three daughters and two sons, only one, Greg, still at home.

Contents

Foreword

If Jesus Christ is the most important person in history—and I believe that He is—then what He taught has to be the most important body of truth ever given to man. Unlike other teachers, Jesus speaks with authority, not from authorities. He never has to appeal to another court, because what He teaches is the final court of appeal. The common people heard Him gladly, and they will so hear Him today if only given the opportunity. That is why I heartily recommend this book to you, because in it the author lets Jesus Christ speak for Himself about the issues that perplex you and me today.

Many writers use the words of Jesus to defend their own ideas, but Stanley Baldwin does not. He presents what Jesus said and then tells you what it means for your life today and how you can put it to work. In other words, this is a *practical* book, not a series of abstract theological studies. The theology is here—plenty of it—but it's the kind of theology that Jesus taught: down-to-earth, personal, practical, and (best of all) exciting. This is not a "book for the quiet hour." Rather, it is a training manual for contemporary Christians who mean business about living for Christ in this critical hour in history.

Best of all, the author knows how to present the teachings of Jesus in a way that does not detract from their simplicity and beauty. An experienced journalist, Stanley Baldwin knows the proper use of illustration, and his writing clarifies instead of clouds the issue. He doesn't try to improve on the Bible; he merely presents the words of Jesus in a way that makes you say, "I never saw *that* before!" And, after all, discovering truth for yourself is the best way to learn.

This is a book you will read again and again, and, I'm sure, refer to often. It will make your Bible more meaningful and your Christian life more enjoyable. Could you ask for much more from a book?

WARREN W. WIERSBE
Moody Church, Chicago, Ill.

Preface

Multiplied scores of volumes have been written about Jesus Christ. Yet few authors, apart from the Gospel writers themselves, have taken the trouble to survey what Jesus actually said and then to present that teaching in a concise and comprehensive manner.

We have books that are broad, surveying the entire life and times of Jesus Christ. Ponderous, massive works, they are eminently valuable but do not focus on His teaching in depth, subject by subject.

We have books that are narrow, examining the parables of Jesus or the prophecies of Jesus or the prayers of Jesus or the Sermon on the Mount. Again, many of these are valuable but fail to give Jesus' comprehensive teaching on various subjects.

Notable among the few authors who have attempted to present the teachings of Jesus per se is G. Campbell Morgan, who wrote *The Teachings of Christ*. Even here, however, we have only Jesus' teachings concerning personalities, sin and salvation, and the Kingdom of God. Important as those categories are, we are left without the definitive teaching of Jesus on such topics as faith, prayer, freedom, the use of money, and other vital subjects.

Remarkably, even the teaching methods of Jesus have often received more attention from authors than His teachings themselves.

It is almost as if people have said. "Jesus? He's the greatest. We will read anything and everything *about* Him, analyze it, discuss it, debate it, and institutionalize it, but don't bother us with what He actually said."

Which brings to mind the poignantly applicable question of Jesus, **"Why call ye Me, Lord, Lord, and *do not the things which I say?"*** (Luke 6:46, KJV) Do what He says? How can we? We haven't bothered to listen. *We in fact do not know what He said.*

But I must not overstate the case. Christians have by no means ignored or been indifferent to the teachings of Jesus. We do care.

We read the Gospels. We study the Word. Nevertheless, when it comes to a serious and comprehensive study of His teachings, we have been strangely inactive.

Some may question the validity of focusing on the teachings of Jesus. "All the Bible is inspired of God, and the words of Jesus are no more inspired, no more authoritative than the rest of Scripture."

This view is only partly correct and is subject to serious misinterpretation. While all the Bible is divinely inspired, some parts are a divinely inspired record of what fallible men have said. And sometimes these fallible men have not spoken truth. The Book of Ecclesiastes is a prime example. Many of its statements are contrary to God's revealed truth because they are—and only purport to be—the views of man "under the sun." They are observations about life as it appears from natural man's viewpoint. Similarly Job contains a dialogue between Job and his friends, in which, though they express themselves convincingly, they are not truly speaking for God.

In the New Testament, the words of Gamaliel are often cited as though they expressed divine truth. Warning the Jewish leaders to be careful how they dealt with the Christians, Gamaliel said, "Leave these men alone! Let them go! For if their purpose or activity is of human origin, it will fail. But if it is from God, you will not be able to stop these men; you will only find yourselves fighting against God" (Acts 5:38-39). But Gamaliel was an unbelieving Jew, and the fact is that many works—false cults, pagan religions, Communism—have grown and flourished for centuries, though they are against all God approves. Even if Gamaliel's words prove true in the absolute long-term sense (everything not of God will at last come to nought), his statement is still worthless in the context in which it is given: namely, that the divine sanction on an enterprise may be judged by the success or failure *we observe* it to have.

Such instances of false statements are uncommon in the New Testament, and it is not our aim to weaken anyone's confidence in the Word of God. Nevertheless, it is necessary to "rightly divide" that Word. We must not attribute to God the statements which He attributes to others.

In any case, it should be beyond all question that the words of Jesus express the distilled truth of God. And it is certainly in order that we should search out these words, take them seriously, and order our lives accordingly. We will find, of course, that they are in harmony with the rest of God's revelation, for truth is always in harmony with truth. But we may also find that we have never before realized what He was saying, perhaps never before realized even that *He has spoken* on some of the particular questions we will be considering.

What Jesus said is forever: **"Heaven and earth will pass away, but *My words* will never pass away"** (Matt. 24:35; Mark 13:31; Luke 21:33).

What Jesus said is the key to successful living: **"Therefore, everyone who hears *these words of Mine* and puts them into practice is like a wise man who built his house on the rock. The rain came down, the streams rose, and the winds blew and beat against that house; yet it did not fall, because it had its foundation on the rock"** (Matt. 7:24-25).

What Jesus said is the key to fellowship with God. **"If anyone loves Me, he will obey *My teaching.* My Father will love him, and We will come to him and make Our home with him. He who does not love Me will not obey My teaching. These words you hear are not My own; they belong to the Father who sent Me"** (John 14:23-24).

What Jesus said is for our daily guidance: **"All this I have spoken while still with you. But the Counselor, the Holy Spirit, whom the Father will send in My name, will teach you all things and will remind you of *everything I have said to you"*** (John 14:25-26).

What Jesus said constitutes our message to others: **"Therefore go and make disciples of all nations . . . teaching them to *obey everything I have commanded you"*** (Matt. 28:19-20).

It seems then, that it is vitally important to know—*What did Jesus say about that?*

1
What Did Jesus Say About . . .
FAITH?

Phil Hayes cherished a dream. He wanted to earn a lot of money, buy a schooner, and sail around the world. No idle dreamer, Phil was the kind of man who seemingly could do anything, once he set his mind to it. His wife described him as the only man in the world who could walk on water. Faith in himself was one thing Phil had in abundance.

Phil's faith got results too. A great success in business, he soon was well on his way to fulfilling his dream. He bought a beautiful 52-foot schooner named the *Astrea,* recruited a crew of four adventurers, and set out on a shakedown cruise to Mexico.

Things began to go sour on the shakedown cruise. The ship developed problems, and soon the crew lost confidence in Phil as skipper and deserted. Phil's wife turned against the idea.

But Phil had faith. No combination of bad breaks was going to deter him now. His dream of a four-year round-the-world cruise was in his grasp, and he was not going to let it slip away. He enlisted a new crew and sailed for Tahiti. Neither Phil Hayes nor any trace of the *Astrea* or its crew was ever seen again despite a long and intensive search by the Coast Guard. Seven years later, Phil Hayes was declared legally dead.*

You won't hear about Phil, who no doubt perished at sea, or

---

* Based on a true story by Lee Hayes, as told to Tom Watson, Jr., *Power For Living,* Dec. 10, 1972. Used by permission of Scripture Press Publications, Inc.

about other similar tragedies, from many present-day cheerleaders for faith. To multitudes of such people, faith is the greatest consumer product since popcorn.

Positive thinkers, faith healers, supersalesman types, politicians, psychologists, preachers—all the would-be good guys have good things to say about faith. It's almost in a category with apple pie, motherhood, and the flag!

For too many people, however, the *object* of faith is largely irrelevant. Only believe strongly enough and what you desire will come to be. Your own subconscious will bring it to pass, or in some mysterious way faith itself will produce the desired result. Or if you believe strongly enough, that being called God, way out in space somewhere, will cause your dreams to come true. Just believe and you will triumph. Simply have faith.

Like Phil?

Jesus talked about faith, but not about this vague faith in faith variety. In fact, a great deal of His teaching about faith serves specifically to clarify *what faith is*—or at least what it must be to have any value.

What Is Faith?

A military man, commander of 100 soldiers, once sought Jesus' help for a servant afflicted with palsy, a condition marked by paralysis or uncontrollable tremors of the affected parts of the body. When Jesus offered to come to the commander's home to help the servant, the officer answered, "Lord, I do not deserve to have You come under my roof. But just say the word, and my servant will be healed" (Matt. 8:8).

What faith! This man believed that Jesus could heal his servant without even going near him. Most people need aids to their faith. They would find it much easier to expect healing if Jesus would lay hands on the man, anoint him with oil, or at least stand over him and pray. "Just say the word and my servant will be healed" expresses sublime faith indeed.

Jesus praised the faith of the officer, saying, *"I tell you the truth, I have not found anyone in Israel with such great faith"* (Matt. 8:10).

The key to the officer's great faith, however, is in his *understanding of authority*. Being a military man, he himself was subject to superior officers, and his men were subject to him. He said, "I tell this one, 'Go,' and he goes; and that one, 'Come,' and he comes. I say to my servant, 'Do this,' and he does it" (Matt. 8:9).

The officer's remarkable faith in Jesus was possible because he understood that Jesus had divine authority. Jesus could speak the word, "Go," and the disease would have to go.

So this was no fuzzy "faith in faith" on the part of the officer. It was a faith in the authority of the Son of God. That's what biblical faith is. The only faith sure to work lasting wonders for the one who believes is a faith that is based on authority or credibility. Otherwise, faith may be only a delusion, a false confidence, and a very costly one at that.

A 70-year-old Chicago woman was walking to the store one morning when a young woman stopped her to ask directions to the public library. She had found two books and wanted to return them. As they talked, the young woman suddenly discovered a stack of $100 bills in one of the books! Before her startled eyes, the woman saw $20,000 produced out of the book.

"What do I do now?" the young woman asked her.

Just then a second young woman happened by. Hearing the whole story, she offered the good news that her lawyer employer had his offices just around the corner. She would ask him what to do.

In a few minutes the lawyer's secretary was back with good news. The women would have to place the $20,000 in a safe deposit box for 60 days, against possible claims by the owner. After that, if unclaimed, it would be theirs!

Meantime, there was one technicality; they would have to put up $4,500 of their own funds as "earnest money." The two younger women excitedly agreed to put up $1,500 apiece. After all, each stood to gain over $6,000. The elderly woman hesitated; she only had $800 in savings.

"That's OK," the lawyer's secretary said. "You were nice enough to let me in on the deal, so I'll put up the extra $700 for you. I mean, what's the difference; I'll get it back, plus a third of the $20,000!"

So the women all went for their funds and returned to the original meeting place, where they pooled the money. The lawyer's secretary said her boss needed to see each of them separately But when the elderly woman went around the corner as she was directed, she couldn't find the lawyer's office. And when she returned to her two young friends, they—and the money—were gone! Without even realizing it, she had put faith in complete strangers, and they had been unworthy of it. It cost her all her savings.

The whole confidence racket is built on misplaced faith. A well-dressed man comes to your door, flashes some identification, and tells you he is investigating possible embezzlement of funds at the savings and loan where you have a deposit. He asks your cooperation in trapping the culprit, emphasizing, of course, that you must not tell anyone lest you ruin the plan. The complex strategy involves your withdrawing your funds, which the "investigator" tells you he will mark and then redeposit through the suspected embezzler. Of course, when he takes the money to mark it, that is the last you see of either him or the money.

People have at times trusted crooked politicians, quack doctors, religious frauds, and false friends. They have been taken in by "free vacation" offers, wonderful "land bargains," home improvements "almost free to you as our way of advertising in your neighborhood," magazine subscriptions for "just the price of postage"—the list is nearly endless.

In all these situations, people have had faith . . . unfortunately. Though nothing was wrong with their faith, it was certainly misplaced. They believed someone who had no credibility.

And many people, like Phil, the schooner skipper, have had too much faith in themselves. Some have launched into their own businesses, confident of success only because of their blissful ignorance of the realities of business life. And they have failed.

Faith is great, but it has to be based on truth if it is to be ultimately beneficial.

Why Believe in Jesus?
That's the complaint some people have against Christianity. They would like to believe it, but they don't think it's believable. "It would be great," one college coed said, "to know I have God on my side, watching over me through life and preparing a glorious destiny in heaven for me hereafter. But I don't want to kid myself."

Jesus doesn't want us to kid ourselves either. He expects us to base our faith on credible evidence. Christianity does require faith but *not blind faith*. Jesus gave strong evidences of His credibility. He said, **"Do not believe Me unless I do what My Father does. But if I do it, even though you do not believe Me, *believe the evidence* of the miracles"** (John 10:37-38).

If a man comes claiming to be God, should we believe him? Certainly not. He is no doubt a fraud or a mental case. But if a man comes claiming to be God and does miracles only God can do, what then? That is a different case. Now, his claim has some credibility.

Jesus reiterated the principle in these words: **"Believe Me when I say that I am in the Father and the Father is in Me; or at least *believe on the evidence* of the miracles themselves"** (John 14:11).

To give further credibility to His claims, Jesus pointed to His foreknowledge. He said concerning His betrayal by Judas, **"I am telling you now before it happens, so that when it does happen you will believe that I am He"** (John 13:19; see also John 14:29).

Yes, Jesus wants us to require a sound basis for faith. Then our faith is more than wishful thinking or self-delusion. Then we can believe with the kind of sublime confidence demonstrated by the military commander whose servant Jesus healed.

Biblical faith, then, is well based. Biblical faith is also *dynamic;* it alters the life of the one who possesses it.

Jesus used a rather unflattering phrase to address His disciples occasionally. He would say, **"O ye of little faith . . . "** (see Matt. 6:30; 8:26; 14:30-31; 16:8).

In every case, He said this to His disciples when they had shown anxiety or fear in their circumstances. Though they were "believers," their faith was not the controlling dynamic in their lives at those moments. They were anxious about their daily needs, or afraid they would perish in a storm on the Sea of Galilee (though He was with them in the boat!), or worried that He was criticizing them for an oversight.

The obvious thrust of Jesus' words when He chided them for little faith at these times is that strong faith would have made them react differently. Faith is not an easy believism but a dynamic conviction that alters the life of the one who believes.

Furthermore, faith, according to Jesus, is a *major element* in right living, not some fringe nicety or a bit of grease on the gears to make life run more smoothly. When He accused the super-religious Pharisees of violating "the weightier matters of the law" in their concern for details, he listed as those more important matters "judgment, mercy, and *faith*" (Matt. 23:23, KJV).

Faith Brings Life

Jesus did not stop with general statements about faith's importance; He specifically detailed the immense and indispensable blessings faith can bring into one's experience. The most important and basic of these is *spiritual life*. He said, **"For God so loved the world that He gave His only begotten Son, that whosoever believeth in Him should not perish but have everlasting life"** (John 3:16, KJV). Note that everlasting life is for "whosoever *believeth*."

He said, **"I tell you the truth, whoever hears My word and *believes Him who sent Me* has eternal life and will not be condemned; he has crossed over from death to life"** (John 5:24).

Some people asked Jesus what they should do to be working acceptably for God unto eternal life. He said, **"The work of God is this: *to believe in the One* whom He has sent"** (John 6:29).

One woman showed the depth of her love and gratitude by pouring out on Jesus' feet a gift of precious ointment. To her, Jesus stated the effective power of faith in the strongest terms. **"Your *faith has saved you*; go in peace"** (Luke 7:50).

Some theologian types wince a bit at those words of Jesus. Had they been there, they might very well have tried to straighten Jesus out on this point. To them, it might seem unfortunate that Jesus spoke as imprecisely as He did, for we know that *faith saves no one*. It is Jesus by His death on the cross who saves men. There is no merit or saving power in faith itself. Faith is merely the hand that receives the proffered gift.

But Jesus splits no theological hairs. Certainly it was His forthcoming work of atonement on the cross that would actually save this woman. But it was faith that *made salvation hers!* And it is faith that makes salvation ours—or unbelief that keeps us outside the kingdom of God. Indeed, our faith will "save us" or we will not be saved at all. **"*If you do not believe* that I am the One I claim to be, you will indeed die in your sins"** (John 8:24).

Faith Brings Blessing

Faith not only brings life, but it also brings the personal fulfillment that makes the Christian life the "more abundant" experience of which Jesus spoke (see John 10:10, KJV).

Jesus expressed an abiding principle when He said, **"According to your faith will it be done to you"** (Matt. 9:29). *The quality of the life we live will be absolutely determined by the degree and kind of faith we have.*

Dr. James D. Mallory puts it this way: "Actually many people have a negative faith. They believe all right, but they believe the wrong things. They believe that they are the way they are because they were 'just born that way.' They believe that they would be simply pretending if they even tried to change. They believe that they will be as they are now until the day they die. Far from lacking faith they have strong faith. And their faith is producing the very negative and destructive things that make them and their loved ones unhappy" (*The Kink and I—a Psychiatrist's Guide to Untwisted Living,* Victor Books, Wheaton, Ill.).

Survey the life and ministry of Jesus Christ and you will see that faith is repeatedly credited for bringing blessing into the lives of those He helped.

A man so sick he had to be carried was brought to Jesus by four friends. They had such faith in Jesus that, when they could not get to Him because of the crowds at the door, they went up on the roof, made an opening, and let the sick man down in front of Christ. "When Jesus *saw their faith,* He said, **'Friend, your sins are forgiven'** " (Luke 5:20).

A woman who had been sick for 12 years had such faith that she was sure she would be healed if she could but touch the hem of Jesus' garment. She managed to get close enough to do just that. "Jesus turned and saw her. **'Take heart, daughter,'** He said, **'your *faith has healed* you'** " (Matt. 9:22).

Another woman, not even an Israelite, was told that she did not qualify for Jesus' help. In language that sounds almost cruel, Jesus implied that she was a "dog" and should not receive the children's (Israel's) bread. Many people then and now, not understanding some seeming harsh treatment from the Lord, take offense at Him. Unlike them, this woman had a faith that could not be denied. She believed Jesus was powerful enough to help and compassionate enough to care, appearances notwithstanding.

Humbly she said, " 'Yes, Lord . . . but even the dogs eat the crumbs that fall from their masters' table.'

"Then Jesus answered, **'Woman you have *great faith!* Your request is granted' "** (Matt. 15:27-28).

Bartimaeus, a blind beggar beside the road, cried out to Jesus as He passed by. Though many told the beggar to be quiet, his faith in Jesus was such that he cried out all the more. Jesus stopped and called the blind man to him. *"Your faith has healed you,"* He told him, and immediately Bartimaeus received his sight (see Mark 10:46-52).

Jesus once healed ten lepers, of whom only one returned to thank Him. To that one, Jesus said, **"Rise and go; your faith has made you well"** (Luke 17:19). This man was made well not only in body but also in soul, while those who were ungrateful never received that fuller and more important blessing of spiritual life. In any case, whatever blessing the leper received, Jesus said it was as a result of faith.

The critically important role of faith is summed up well in what Jesus said to Martha, as recorded in John 11:40. Her brother Lazarus had died, and Jesus was about to restore him to life. Martha did not want the tomb opened because the decaying body would make a stench. Jesus said, **"Did I not tell you that *if you believe, you would see* the glory of God?"** So often, we want to reverse that process. If we could see the glory of God, then we would believe. But faith on our part is a prerequisite to seeing and experiencing God's blessings. And without faith it is impossible to please God (see Heb. 11:6).

Faith Brings Power

Faith not only brings us salvation and multiplied blessings but it gives us power as well. " **'Have faith in God,'** Jesus answered. **'I tell you the truth, if anyone says to this mountain, "Go, throw yourself into the sea," and *does not doubt in his heart but believes* that what he says will happen, it will be done for him. Therefore I tell you, whatever you ask for in prayer, believe that you will receive it, and it will be yours' "** (Mark 11:22-24).

This mountain-moving promise of Jesus seems plainly incredible. Of course, the fact is that a rational person knows it is impossible for a mountain to obey a man's orders to cast itself into the sea. Therefore, he could hardly command such a thing expecting *without a doubt* it would happen.

In this sense, these words of Jesus are reminiscent of the Scandinavian fable about the gold mill. In one version of the fable, a skipper acquires the wonderful machine which grinds out gold on command and takes it to sea with him. Two things go wrong with his plans to make himself enormously wealthy. First, he fails to learn how to stop the machine. Second, he has been warned that the mill will grind out salt as well as gold. When he commands it to produce gold, he must not even think of salt, or it will produce salt. Poor fellow. Try as he will, when he turns on the machine the forbidden thought of salt leaps to his mind. Not knowing how to stop the machine, he watches helplessly as the salt fills and sinks his ship. The mill has been on the bottom of the ocean relentlessly grinding out salt ever since, and that, dear children, is how the ocean became so salty.

Surely Jesus was not playing a mental game—a "don't think salt"/"don't doubt" trick? No, but neither was He giving lessons in mountain moving. What He was doing was expressing the almost limitless and incredible power of faith.

And Scripture teaches the converse truth as well. As faith energizes and empowers, so unbelief cripples and confines. Jesus' disciples were unable to help a demonized boy, but Jesus instantaneously healed him. When the disciples asked why they were so powerless, He replied, **"Because you have so little faith"** (Matt. 17:20).

Unfortunately, our unbelief can restrict the power of God Himself to work on our behalf, since He limits Himself to responding to our faith (see Hebrews 11:6). Thus we read concerning Jesus' hometown, Nazareth, "And He did not do many miracles there because of their lack of faith" (Matt. 13:58). Do those same tragic words describe our lives? Do we know little of Jesus' power in our lives because we will not believe?

But what if we do believe? What miracles will happen?

Who knows? The resourcefulness, grace, and power of God are beyond our imagination. But whatever else may happen, the most important result is described by Jesus Himself. **"If a man is thirsty, let him come to Me and drink. *Whoever believes in Me,* as the Scripture has said, streams of living water will flow from within him"** (John 7:37-38).

The symbolic language confuses some, but the truth is a powerful and compelling one. People are thirsty. They have all kinds of unresolved needs and desires. Often these are but an expression of the most basic need of all—for spiritual reality. Jesus said such people could come to Him *and drink*. The supply of our innermost needs will be met in Jesus. But more than this, Jesus gives believers an abundant, exhaustless, *inner supply* of fresh, running water so they need never be thirsty again and indeed may overflow with life-giving refreshment to those around them.

Scripture tells us that the "streams of living water" Jesus promised within us represent the Spirit "whom those *who believed* in Him were later to receive" (John 7:39).

So God gives the fullness of His Spirit to those who believe in Jesus, and the Spirit within us is a never-failing supply of life and satisfaction.

Should someone say, "I believe in Jesus, but I have not known this stream of living water within," we'd be compelled to reply, "Whom shall we believe? You or Jesus? Since we believe Him, we must conclude something is wrong with your faith. Perhaps your belief is a mere intellectual assent. Vital faith *claims the promises* of God and stands upon them. The promise of God before us here guarantees "springs of living water" within. How can you have faith and still not claim this promise for your own life and experience?

Faith also brings us power for service. Jesus said, **"I tell you the truth, anyone who has faith in Me will do what I have been doing. He will do even greater things than these, because I am going to the Father"** (John 14:12).

This is no appeal to sensationalism. We aren't supposed to try to eclipse the great miracles Jesus performed by doing even more spectacular ones. The *greatest work* of Jesus was clearly in serving and helping people, particularly with their spiritual needs. He said repeatedly that giving service was the greatest thing we could do (see Matt. 20:25-28; 23:11; Luke 22:25-27). His own life was cut short (**"I am going to the Father"**), so many of Jesus' disciples have won more converts, taught more disciples, helped more unfortunates than He did. But it is faith that enables people to do these great works. Otherwise, we are too busy meeting our own needs, too inadequate to contribute greatly to anyone else.

How to Have Faith

It would be tragic to sing the praises of faith and never explain how to have it. Jesus would not do such a thing.

Jesus' parable of the seed and the sower reveals that faith comes from hearing the Word of God. **"This is the meaning of the parable: The seed is the Word of God. Those along the path are the ones who hear, and then the devil comes and takes away the Word from their hearts,** *so that they cannot believe and be saved"* (Luke 8:11-12).

Faith needs to be generated by and nourished on the Word of God. So much so that one "cannot believe and be saved" without it. This we should have realized, for we already learned from Jesus that faith is belief based on evidence (see p. 14). It is the Bible that gives us this credible information on which to base our faith.

Jesus also taught that faith can be purified and strengthened by trial. Before his denial of the Lord, Peter believed sincerely in Jesus. But he also had a lot of self-confidence, even arrogance. It was hard to tell where his faith left off and his arrogance began. Hard even for Peter to know how much of his strength came from faith in Christ and how much from faith in Peter.

Apparently the Lord decided to let Satan put Peter through severe temptation that his faith might be purified. He said, **"Simon, Simon, Satan has asked to sift you all as wheat. But I have prayed for you, Simon, that your faith may not fail"** (Luke 22:31-32). As it turned out, though *Peter did fail* (he denied the Lord three times within the next 24 hours), his faith survived and became far purer and ultimately stronger than it had ever been before. The Lord may, and most likely will, allow our faith to be tested also. If our faith is real, it will survive. And, after the experience passes, we will have even more faith than before.

Faith Is By Choice

It is important to realize that faith also has a volitional element. That is, we may simply choose or will to believe.

A popular television series called "To Tell the Truth" presented three individuals all claiming the same identity. Two of them lied as convincingly as they could in answer to the questions of panel members attempting to identify the real character. Panelists had to *choose* whom to believe. Often, one can and does choose whom he will believe.

Senator Edward Kennedy was involved in a compromising situation at Chappaquiddick. He was alone with a young woman, not his wife, late at night, in an isolated place. His car missed a bridge, though the road was familiar to Kennedy, and the woman drowned in the submerged car, despite his alleged attempts to rescue her. Everybody had to choose whether to believe Kennedy's version of the incident or not to believe it. Their choices were determined largely by their confidence or lack of it in him as a person. Then, too, some people (his wife, his political supporters) had reasons for preferring to believe him. Others (political opponents, personal enemies) had reasons to prefer not to believe him.

We are constantly making choices to believe or not believe in our day-to-day lives. We hear various accounts from our friends and associates—accounts of everything from their successes at fishing or on the golf course to the great deal they got or loss they suffered in buying a dinner, a car, or a house. As we hear all these accounts, we are inwardly believing or disputing them. We would almost stake our lives on the reports of some people because we trust them. We believe them even if there is considerable evidence to the contrary, or even if they give us a stranger-than-fiction story. Other people might tell us something quite believable in itself. Because we view them as unreliable empty talkers, however, we doubt that they are telling us the truth.

Thus our belief or lack of it says something about the relationship that exists between us and the source of the information. That is why unbelief as it relates to God becomes a moral matter. Not to believe is a sin. It impugns the character of God, calling Him untrustworthy. It is an insult to the Deity.

The Bible says that Jesus rebuked His disciples for their unbelief. One such occasion was after His resurrection when they would not believe those who claimed they had seen Him alive. "He rebuked them for their lack of faith and their stubborn refusal to believe those who had seen Him after He had risen" (Mark 16:14).

Rebuke is appropriate only when there has been wrongdoing. Jesus would not have rebuked the disciples if they had not had a choice about whether to believe. They chose not to believe. It was a "stubborn refusal," and as such it was blameworthy.

Thomas was particularly recalcitrant. He said, "Unless I see the nail marks in His hands and put my finger where the nails were, and put my hand into His side, I will not believe it" (John 20:25).

At least Thomas was honest in his description of the situation. He did not say "I *cannot* believe it," but "I *will not* believe it."

Jesus gave Thomas the evidence he demanded, but was clearly displeased with him. Appearing to Thomas, He said, **"Put your finger here; see My hands. Reach out your hand and put it into My side. Stop doubting and believe"** (John 20:27).

When Thomas thereupon acknowledged the reality of Christ's resurrection, Jesus said, **"Because you have seen Me, you have believed; blessed are those who have not seen and yet have believed"** (John 20:29).

Stubborn unbelief, choosing not to believe when we could just as well choose to believe, is an offense to God. We are not talking here about blind faith. We have already said that biblical faith must be built on credible evidence. We don't need any more people like those described by one Christian man of science. He commented that many Christians believe things they *know* are not so. He referred to Christians who make no attempt to integrate faith and intellect, who are afraid to examine the tenets of their faith.

But Thomas had credible evidence even before the Lord appeared to him. He had the testimony of all the other disciples, who had personally seen the risen Lord a week previously. These were men whose integrity was unquestioned, personal friends of Thomas. He could have chosen to believe them, and he should have.

The great trouble with the inclination to unbelief is that it can easily be *the determining factor* in life. If a person *chooses* not to believe, it can well nigh be impossible to bring him to faith, Thomas being quite the exception here.

"A man convinced against his will.

Is of the same opinion still."

Jesus described a man in hell pleading that someone be sent to warn his five brothers lest they also end up in hell. The reply: "They have Moses and the Prophets [the Bible]; let them listen to them" (Luke 16:29).

The man in hell argues that they will not heed the Bible but that if one rose from the dead to warn them, they would repent.

The reply: "If they do not listen to Moses and the Prophets, they will not be convinced even if someone rises from the dead" (Luke 16:31).

Our first inclination may be to agree with the man in hell. Certainly if one rose from the dead, his warning would be heeded! But Jesus said no. People have in the Bible all the evidence they need *if they are willing* to believe and repent. If they are unwilling, no amount of evidence will convince them. They can claim the resurrected man was never really dead, or that they had been hallucinating when they thought he appeared to them, or that it was a clever trick by a religious impersonator, or. . . . The resourcefulness of the human mind can always come up with some justification for refusing to believe.

The proof of Jesus' correctness on this point lies in the fact that when God actually did send Someone back from the grave (Jesus Himself), those who were determined not to believe attempted to explain away His resurrection (see Matt. 28:11-15).

"Blessed are those who have not seen and yet have believed," said Jesus (John 20:29). That is a blessing we can choose today. On the basis of the evidence, we can trust in Christ. We can live by faith daily and receive the blessings God delights to give to those who trust Him. We can have within us a river of living water not only to satisfy our own needs but to flow out to others.

"According to your faith be it unto you."

2
What Did Jesus Say About . . .
SIN?

Cal Coolidge, a man of few words, was asked by his wife as he returned from church what the minister preached about.

"Sin," said Cal.

"Well, what did he have to say about it?"

"He was against it."

Most people think they already know what Jesus said about sin. They figure He was against it. And no doubt He was. But some things Jesus said have been used to justify sin.

Take, for example, the following passage: **"What goes into a man's mouth does not make him 'unclean,' but what comes out of his mouth, that is what makes him 'unclean' "** (Matt. 15:11).

This statement by Jesus really unhinged the Pharisees. And it rather puzzled the disciples too. They figured it made a lot of difference what you put in your mouth.

Jesus explained. **"Don't you see that whatever enters the mouth goes into the stomach and then out of the body? But the things that come out of the mouth come from the heart, and these make a man 'unclean.' For out of the heart come evil thoughts, murder, adultery, sexual immorality, theft, false testimony, slander. These are what make a man 'unclean,' but eating with unwashed hands does not make him 'unclean' "** (Matt. 15:17-20).

This is undoubtedly the favorite Scripture passage of some people, particularly those who like to indulge in the consumption

24

of various commodities that others may consider sinful. Individuals who never revealed an acquaintance with anything else in all the Scripture have cited this passage to me.

How literally, and in how absolute a sense, are we to understand Jesus' words? Is it really true that nothing that enters a man's mouth defiles him? Did Jesus intend His words to be taken as justification for smoking and for drinking alcoholic beverages? Some would say so. But most would hesitate to press the rule further. For example, did Jesus intend to justify drinking to excess? Gluttony? How about ingesting various drugs without restraint? Smoking marijuana?

If nothing entering the mouth can defile, is it OK to swallow a lethal overdose of sleeping pills or strychnine or lye?

The fact is, of course, that it does matter what we ingest and what we inhale. It is a matter of both practical and moral concern. (The two usually go together.) Jesus Himself warned against overindulgence in eating and drinking (Matt. 24:49; Luke 21:34). Yet both overeating and drunkenness relate to what enters the mouth.

So why did Jesus say what He did in Matthew 15?

Of course, as the context reveals, Jesus was specifically saying that *eating with unwashed hands* was not sinful. But He also no doubt meant the principle to be carried further than that. The question is, how far? And why did He express Himself in such a way as to permit people to abuse His teaching, to carry it to such extremes as to excuse sin?

In a real sense, Jesus' teachings are moral tests in themselves. What a person does with the teachings of Jesus reveals a lot about the person. If one wants a justification for his sin, he will seize on statements such as this one with a vengeance. But if he is a seeker for truth, he will make a sincere effort to determine exactly what Jesus meant. By the nature of his response, he reveals what kind of person he is. That is no doubt one reason Jesus spoke in the puzzling way He sometimes did.

The Nature of Sin

Though Jesus' very words were perhaps a moral test, He was no doubt also expressing a great and basic principle about the nature of sin. It is, generally speaking, not a matter of outward habits but of inward character. And it is, particularly, not a matter of observing rules which have no intrinsic moral content . . . such as washing one's hands before eating.

The trouble is that rules which have been deeply engrained in a person's conscience assume the force of moral law whether they have any intrinsic moral content or not. Jesus knew there was nothing sinful about eating with unwashed hands, but the Pharisees did not. In fact, they were "knocked breathless" by Jesus' statement, according to the Williams translation of Matthew 15:12.

All their lives, the Pharisees had understood it was sinful to eat with unwashed hands. This conviction was not based on hygienic considerations. They didn't know there were such things as germs. It was simply an old tradition (v. 2) that they had accepted without analyzing. But it was deeply engrained.

If we were to explore all the implications of Jesus' remarks on this occasion, we might hear Him saying that we need to examine our scruples and "sacred convictions" with an open mind to see whether the things we have always been taught to condemn are indeed sinful. If we have nothing but the "tradition of the elders" to support our condemnation of a practice, we are on thin ice, however certain our conditioned consciences may be of the unquestioned guilt-worthiness of the act. In any case, the central truth Jesus was attempting to communicate is that the heart, not merely the hands, must be kept clean.

Sin is an inward tendency toward or preference for evil. Wrong actions (*sins*) are outward expressions of this inward tendency.

Jesus repeatedly emphasized this. Here, He says it in so many words: **"Out of the heart come evil thoughts, murder, adultery, sexual immorality, theft, false testimony, slander"** (Matt. 15:19).

Elsewhere, He talked about the same thing under the symbol of a tree and its fruit. **"Likewise every good tree bears good fruit, but a bad tree bears bad fruit. A good tree cannot bear bad fruit, and a bad tree cannot bear good fruit"** (Matt. 7:17-18).

Some people are only concerned about fruit (actions). Jesus said the fruit is going to correspond with the tree (nature or heart). Man's sin shows he has spiritual heart trouble (see Jer. 17:9).

The Evidence of Sin
Jesus said it is not what enters the mouth but what comes out of it

that defiles a man (Matt. 15:11). The mouth reveals most clearly the condition of the heart.

A man may be lustful without ever assaulting a woman. He may fear the penalty of the law, or public disgrace, or the consequences to his family. Or he may simply lack opportunity to fulfill his sensual desires. But a lustful man is not likely to keep it from showing in his speech. Thousands of respectable family men who behave themselves sexually, to say nothing of schoolboys who are inexperienced sexually, wallow in lust verbally. Their tongues accurately index their hearts though their behavior does not.

A man may be profane and blasphemous without ever desecrating a local church, tearing up a Bible, or publicly opposing God. The irreverence for God in his heart appears in his speech. God's name is outrageously profaned every day by people who do not otherwise show themselves hostile to true religion.

A malicious racist may never pump anyone full of bullets, but you may be quite sure his malice will show in his speech. As Jesus put it, **"Out of the overflow of the heart the mouth speaks. The good man brings good things out of the good stored up in him, and the evil man brings evil things out of the evil stored up in him"** (Matt. 12:34-35).

If a person wants to know what subjects are dealt with in a textbook, he can simply turn to the index and find them listed there. One might never guess from the title everything that is in the book. One might even scan the book for a long time without perceiving all of the contents. But if the index is good, it will soon tell you whether or not a certain subject is treated in the book.

Just so, the tongue is an index of a person's heart. The appearance of a person may deceive you. Even a casual acquaintance with him might mislead you. If you want to know what is in the heart, just check the speech.

This may be threatening to us. We might fear that someone will hear us say something wrong and jump to the conclusion that we are not what we should be. If someone does, that will be one hasty conclusion that is correct!

Do we think it alarming that people may judge us by our speech? What shall we think, then, when we read that God will definitely judge us on that basis? **"But I tell you that men will have to give account on the day of judgment for every careless word they have spoken. For by your words you will**

be acquitted, and by your words you will be condemned" (Matt. 12:36-37).

This warning has often been misunderstood. My Sunday School teacher told me as a teenager that an "idle" word (as the King James Version renders *careless*) is a word that does no work. She made God sound like a tyrant who was busy recording all my small talk, jesting, or casual conversation to hold me accountable for it later. Even as a youth, I instinctively recoiled from such a concept of God. I thought God would not be so austere as to begrudge me a few words that weren't doing their share of work.

Since then, I have decided that if God is going to punish people for speaking unnecessary words, we are all in a lot of trouble. As an editor, it's my work to delete unnecessary words from other people's writings. After doing editorial work a while, you even find yourself editing people's speech. Believe me, people use a lot of idle words. Rare is the piece of writing that cannot be improved by having a full third of the words deleted. And speech is worse. I doubt that God is going to shake the unedited copy of a lifetime of talking in people's faces and say, "Now, about those idle words . . . ."

If this were what Jesus meant, we might do well to take an oath of silence. We wouldn't be much good in a world dependent on communication, but we'd have a lot less to give account for in the judgment!

I have concluded that Jesus meant that our speech is such an accurate index of our hearts that even idle words reveal what we are and are therefore appropriate evidence on which to judge us. It is not that a man should never engage in jesting or small talk. What kind of life would that be? What kind of God would make such demands? But even my jesting and small talk reveal my character. Are my jokes irreverent or smutty? Is my small talk malicious or profane? Every idle word I speak will be admissible evidence of my character before the judgment bar of God because I am speaking out of the abundance of my heart. Nothing can come out that is not resident within.

A sharp-tongued young woman was justifying herself to a friend. "I suppose I shouldn't have said it, but if you knew the aggravation to which I was subjected, you'd understand."

"If you were carrying a pail of water and someone jostled you, what would spill from the pail?" her friend asked.

"Why, water, of course."

"And if you were carrying a pail of acid and someone jostled you, what would spill?"

"Why, acid, of course."

"The only thing that can spill out of your mouth when you are aggravated is what you are carrying in your heart. The spilling might be someone else's fault; the content is yours."

So Jesus' teaching is clear. Sin is an inward matter of the heart and the best spiritual electrocardiogram, the best indicator of your heart's condition is your speech.

The Power of Sin

Jesus said, **"I tell you the truth, everyone who sins is a slave to sin"** (John 8:34). A person ordinarily views his sin as an expression of independence, not slavery. The law says, "Thou shalt not." The person says, "I shall too." He sees this violation of the law as a matter of personal freedom to do as he pleases rather than to submit to the dictates of another.

This view of sin is a great deception, according to Jesus. The person who sins is not finding or expressing freedom. He is embracing slavery.

How is this so?

We said previously that sin is an inward tendency toward or preference for evil. When this tendency is expressed in action, it creates strong behavior patterns. The act reinforces the inclination. It confirms in the character what has already been a leaning of the heart. Now the person has not only an inward tendency toward evil but a behavior pattern, a habit, of expressing that evil. Obviously, as this pattern continues, a person will become less and less able to resist doing evil.

This condition of slavery may exist undetected for a long time. If the person *wants* to live a certain way, if he wants to express a sinful life-style, he has no way of knowing whether or not he is in fact enslaved by the habit. Only if and when he wants to change does he learn he is not free.

For example, a person who smokes because he wants to never knows how strongly the habit holds him. But if he decides to quit, he soon learns whether or not he is enslaved. Usually he finds that he cannot quit without a struggle. He is not totally free to smoke or not smoke. He can stop only by paying a price.

I cite smoking as an example not because it is such a great sin but because it offers a graphic picture of enslavement and is one with which many people can identify. I could as well talk about lust or pride or lying or self-pity or stealing.

When a person *realizes his sin is destroying him,* the moment of truth arrives. And sin does destroy people, though there is not always a cancer warning on the box. Lying destroys a man's credibility and self respect. Stealing destroys a man's social acceptability and initiative. Self-pity blots out the sunlight of life and drives away friends. Sooner or later, often much later, people realize that the things God forbids as sinful are things that hurt them. (Of course, that is why a loving God forbade them in the first place.)

Realizing the destructive nature of a particular sin does not enable a person to stop committing that sin, but it is likely to make him *want* to stop. Then is his moment of truth. He learns he cannot stop. He discovers the truth of Jesus' words: **"Everyone who sins is a slave to sin."**

With the Apostle Paul, it was covetousness. "I would not have known what it was to covet if the law had not said, 'Do not covet.' But sin, seizing the opportunity afforded by the commandment, produced in me every kind of covetous desire" (Rom. 7:7-8).

As Paul tried to live as a Christian, he discovered he was enslaved to many other sins also, both of commission and omission. "For what I want to do I do not do, but what I hate I do. . . . For I have the desire to do what is good, but I cannot carry it out. . . . What a wretched man I am! Who will rescue me from this body of death?" (Rom. 7:15, 18, 24)

Mika Banzako was a thief. He stole from everyone, even his family and friends. In prison he stole from fellow inmates and from the guards. At last the Zairian (formerly Belgian Congo) prison officials resorted to an ancient punishment: they cut off the thief's arm.

When Mika was released, he went into a new area where he was unknown and vowed never to be caught again. Soon he was arrested for burgling the house of a government official. The next day after he was imprisoned, the warden summoned him. A new guard from Mika's former prison had informed about him. "If we hear of even one case of your stealing while you are in my prison, we will cut off your other arm," the warden threatened.

For many days the warden's words echoed in Mika's ears. And for many days he did not steal. He bit his lip and ran in the other direction when an opportunity came for picking pockets or taking tools. At night he covered his eyes and shuddered at what might happen if he were caught once more.

But the time came, as Mika knew it would, when he began stealing again—pocket knives, money, wrist watches. Mika Banzako was just as much a thief as ever. And he was caught. Mika fainted when he heard the warden announce that his remaining arm was to be amputated.

After his eventual release, amazingly, Mika still did not stop stealing. With no hands, he began to steal with his mouth!

In Mika's case, enslavement to the sin of stealing was finally broken. He became a Christian. When the evangelist asked for those wishing to receive Christ to raise their hands, Mika was frustrated, having no hand to raise. But he worked his way to the front of the congregation until he was noticed by the preacher and was led to faith in Christ.*

Mika represents a vivid example of what Jesus said: **"Everyone who sins is a slave of sin."** But Jesus also said on the same occasion, **"If you hold to My teaching, you are really My disciples. Then you will know the truth, and the truth will set you free. So if the Son sets you free, you will be free indeed"** (John 8:31-32, 36). Sin enslaves, but a person can be freed from that slavery by becoming a disciple of Jesus Christ, as Mika was freed from being a thief.

Sanctions Against Sin

Freedom from sin's power comes only when Jesus Christ sets one free. However, God has built deterrents to sin into the very fabric of life, even in a wicked and fallen world that has many inducements to sin. These sanctions tend to check people from unbridled pursuit of sin because of the penalty involved. They also tend to produce the personal desperation and the disaffection with sin that cause people to seek deliverance through Christ.

Jesus used these divine sanctions against sin to warn people away from it and toward commitment to Him. On one occasion,

---

* Adapted from "No Hand to Raise," a true story by Hal Olsen in *FreeWay,* July 29, 1973. Used by permission of Scripture Press Publications, Inc.

He healed a pitiful, friendless cripple who had been 38 years an invalid. Afterward He told him, **"See, you are well again. Stop sinning or something worse may happen to you"** (John 5:14). What a sanction against sin! What a chilling warning! It is difficult to imagine how anything *could* be worse than the condition that man had already endured. But Jesus, the very One who healed him, told him that was exactly what might take place.

This is not to say that all sickness and misfortune is punishment from God for one's personal sins. Jesus specifically told His disciples that a man born blind was not in that condition because of either his sin or that of his parents (John 9:1-3). Nevertheless, much suffering and sickness is a direct or indirect result of one's personal sins, and God wants us to realize that.

As inadequate a deterrent as the warnings on the packages of sin may be, they are far better than nothing. We have previously described how sanctions against sin check people from committing sinful acts though their speech reveals that their hearts are defiled. So the sanctions do restrain overt sin.

Also, a good many people have been converted after God has shown them where sin is leading. They have seen themselves as physically debilitated, morally bankrupt, and socially worthless. God has told them in the silent language of their own hearts that this is the end. It is Christ or else.

The Unpardonable Sin

Sanctions against sin are inadequate in themselves to save a person (as the armless Mika testifies). Christ alone can break sin's bondage and set us free. Therefore, the greatest sin is to reject Christ.

Certainly most people do not view their lack of Christian faith as a sin in itself. Many would resent even the suggestion. The natural man may feel guilty about breaking the Ten Commandments. His conscience may accuse him if he steals or lies or if he even thinks of committing murder or adultery. But the conscience of a natural man does not ordinarily impose guilt upon him for lack of Christian commitment.

Jesus said concerning the Holy Spirit, **"When He comes, He will prove the world wrong about sin and righteousness and judgment: about sin, because men do not believe in Me"** (John 16:8-9).

Note that the particular sin of which the Holy Spirit convicts the world is *not believing in Jesus*. It requires the work of the Holy Spirit to do this, for man does not consider unbelief particularly sinful unless the Holy Spirit produces that conviction.

Another reason the Holy Spirit focuses His conviction of sin on unbelief is that unbelief is the sin of sins, the one sin that prevents the forgiveness of all others.

Jesus said, **"I tell you, every sin and blasphemy will be forgiven men, but the blasphemy against the Spirit will not be forgiven. Anyone who speaks a word against the Son of Man will be forgiven, but anyone who speaks against the Holy Spirit will not be forgiven, either in this age or in the age to come"** (Matt. 12:31-32).

This unpardonable sin—the blasphemy against the Holy Spirit— has puzzled and troubled many. Some sensitive souls have suffered much because they imagine they may have committed this sin. One girl wrote, "As soon as I heard this Scripture, the devil put terrible words against the Holy Spirit into my mind. Have I committed the unpardonable sin?"

Obviously, she had not. Jesus said that **"anyone who *speaks* against the Holy Spirit will not be forgiven"** (v. 32). The girl would have had to accept the devil-suggested thoughts and have given them expression through her speech to fulfill the description of the unpardonable sin.

Incidentally, whoever heard anyone speak against the Holy Spirit? The names of God and Jesus Christ are often profaned, but I never heard the name of the Holy Spirit on profane lips.

However, Jesus no doubt had something more in mind than profanity when He spoke about the sin against the Holy Spirit. The context indicates that maliciously attributing to Satan the work of the Holy Spirit is what Jesus condemned. Actually, there is probably only one unforgivable sin and that is to reject Jesus Christ finally. When the Holy Spirit convicts a person that he should trust in Christ, and he deliberately and *finally* refuses, that is blaspheming the Holy Spirit.

I say *finally* because many people have rejected Jesus Christ and later received Him and been forgiven. But if one finally rejects Christ, he can never be forgiven for he has rejected the very means of forgiveness.

Most municipalities have a fire code for public buildings. The code requires adequate exits which must not be blocked. It may also require lighted exit signs, automatic sprinklers, alarm systems, fire extinguishers at strategic points, fire doors or walls that will resist burn-through for a specified length of time, etc.

Any violation of the fire code is, of course, a "sin" against the fire authority. But if the building should burn while full of people, only one of these violations would be an unpardonable sin—*to have the exits blocked*. Even if the building burned to the ground, all could be saved if they used the exits. But if the building were consumed by flames with the people in it, adherence to the other provisions of the code would avail nothing.

Just so, Jesus is the exit from condemnation for sin. And He is the only exit. To reject Jesus is to seal oneself in a burning building that is destined utterly to perish.

The Spirit convicts of the sin of not believing in Jesus because that is the fatal sin, unforgivable if the unbelief is final.

But is this what Jesus meant when he spoke of blaspheming the Holy Spirit? I believe so. Suppose the Holy Spirit has done His work, convincing a person of the sin of not believing in Jesus. For that person to deliberately and finally choose to continue in unbelief is to sin against the Holy Spirit and to cut himself off forever from the possibility of forgiveness.

What a frightening possibility!

It ought to make every non-Christian run, not walk, to the nearest—and only—exit, faith in Jesus Christ.

3
What Did Jesus Say About . .
The WORD of GOD?

A story is told of a devout father whose son was studying for the ministry. The son chose to go to Europe for an advanced degree, and the father worried that he would be spoiled of his simple faith by sophisticated unbelieving professors. "Don't let them take Jonah away from you," he admonished, figuring the swallowed-by-a-great-fish story might be the first part of the Bible to go.

Two years later when the son returned, the father asked, "Do you still have Jonah in your Bible?"

The son laughed. "Jonah! That story isn't even in *your* Bible."

"It certainly is! What do you mean?"

"It's not in your Bible. Go ahead, show it to me."

The old man fumbled through his Bible looking for the Book of Jonah but couldn't find it. At last he checked the table of contents for the proper page. When he turned there, he discovered the three pages comprising Jonah had been carefully cut from his Bible.

"I did it before I went away," said the son. "What's the difference whether I lose the Book of Jonah through pseudo-sophistication or you lose it through neglect?"

Some people deny or doubt that the Bible is the Word of God. Others say that it is indeed the Word of God, but they never bother to consider its teachings, whether from Jonah or any other part. They do not form their opinions or govern their decisions by God's Word.

There is not a dime's worth of difference between denying the Bible and ignoring it. The only difference is in what people *say* they believe. In reality, neither those who deny or those who ignore the Bible believe it is God's Word to them, absolute, infallible, and the *sine qua non* of life.

Jesus did not generally move in such circles. Jesus lived among people who took the Word of God somewhat more seriously than that. But even among what we might call Bible people, the Word of God suffers. People tend either to circumvent the Word of God somehow or practically to worship it. Both attitudes are wrong. And both can be very subtle and deceptive.

One chief way people circumvent the Word of God is by attaching equal or actually superior authority to tradition. Jesus encountered this often. Once He told the Pharisees, **"You have let go of the commands of God and are holding on to the traditions of men"** (Mark 7:8). The particular distortion Jesus referred to is dealt with in detail in the chapter on money.

It is easy for us to attach divine authority to some traditional prejudice of our own, especially if the tradition has been engrained in us from our youth (see page 26). We must honestly examine all our convictions in the light of the Word of God. Otherwise we may find ourselves "contending for the truth" with all the zeal of a Pharisee when, in fact, our position is contrary to God's Word and God's will.

The error at the other extreme—practically worshiping the Word of God—may seem an unlikely possibility. It is, however, more common and more a threat than we might think. This error will be dealt with at length later in this chapter.

Absolute Authority

Jesus taught that the Word of God is absolute and final and cannot possibly fail.

"Do not think that I have come to abolish the Law or the Prophets; I have not come to abolish them but to fulfill them. I tell you the truth, until heaven and earth disappear, not the smallest letter, not the least stroke of a pen, will by any means disappear from the Law until everything is accomplished. Anyone who breaks one of the least of these commandments and teaches others to do the same will be called least in the kingdom of heaven, but whoever practices and teaches these commands will be called great in the kingdom of heaven" (Matt. 5:17-19).

Jesus said a great deal in a small space when He spoke the foregoing words! Obviously, He took the Scriptures (here called *Law* and *Prophets*) very seriously. He certainly would not have agreed with those who see them as the speculations of idle dreamers. Nor even with those who view them as the best thoughts of godly men. He considered the Scriptures to be the Word of God, the least detail of which was divinely ordained. As He said on a later occasion, **"The Scripture cannot be broken"** (John 10:35).

Jesus said all the Law and Prophets would be *fulfilled*. On this point endless debate centers. Some who are zealous for the Law tell us in commenting on this passage that heaven and earth have by no means disappeared yet, that all Scripture has not yet been fulfilled, and that the Law is still binding on us today. Others who are zealous for grace tell us that the Law (if not the Prophets) was totally fulfilled in Christ. Having been thus "filled full," the Law has no more application to us as Christians.

Both sides have some truth.

Jesus did fulfill the Law. He alone kept the commandments perfectly. (He also often pointed out that events in His life were happening **"to fulfill what is written in their Law"**—John 15:25; see also John 17:12, 18:9.) Because He fulfilled the Law and His perfect righteousness is put to our account when we receive Him by faith, the Law has no more power to demand our death for disobedience. "God made Him who had no sin to be sin for us, so that in Him we might become the righteousness of God" (2 Cor. 5:21). So we are saved by grace through faith. The works of the Law have nothing whatever to do with it (see Eph. 2:8-9). "For we maintain that a man is justified *by faith apart from observing the Law"* (Rom. 3:28).

All of this, however, does not mean the Law of God has no more relevance to our lives. True, the Law is not our means of justification. It is, however, an expression of the will of our Lord. Even more basic, it is a reflection of His very nature. God does not now approve adultery, stealing, profanity, idolatry, and the other acts forbidden by the Law. They were wrong *before* the Ten Commandments were inscribed on stone. They were wrong all during the centuries from Moses to Christ. They have been equally wrong from Christ's time until now. And they will always be wrong.

Conceivably a person can be a Christian and hold that the standards of the Law no longer apply to him and others. But such a man, Jesus said, **"will be called least in the kingdom of heaven, but whoever practices and teaches these commands will be called great in the kingdom of heaven"** (Matt. 5:19).

"Saved by grace" Christians need always to remember, as the Apostle Paul said, that though we cannot keep the Law in our own strength "the righteous requirements of the Law [can] be fully met in us, who do not live according to our sinful nature but according to the Spirit" (Rom. 8:4).

Certainly, Jesus came to fulfill the Law. However, He came not only to fulfill it *for* us but *in* us. How could it be otherwise? Do we think the Holy One becomes less holy when He comes to dwell in our hearts?

Spiritual Truth

While the Word of God is absolute and binding, it is not a dead letter which may be satisfied by slavish conformity to its commands. Even if a man could observe every detail of the Law to the letter, he still might not have met God's requirements for righteousness.

Jesus made this clear in His commentary on the Law, which follows His words about its authority that we have been considering. An interesting and significant pattern develops as Jesus specifically takes up some of the Old Testament commandments. He begins by saying, **"You have heard that it was said . . ."** and then He cites one of the commandments (see Matt. 5:21, 27, 33). He follows by saying, **"But I tell you . . ."** and then He brings forth the underlying principle, the spiritual truth that lies behind the commandment (see Matt. 5:22, 28, 34).

Take the command against murder (v. 21). The positive principle behind that is *good will toward others*. Murder results from hatred, malice, ill will, a negative attitude toward others. Thus, if one does no murder but harbors ill will, he has violated the spirit of the commandment. And he is *guilty*, for the Word of God is not the letter only but the spirit.

God commanded His people to avoid adultery (v. 27). Jesus said the spirit of that law prohibits entertaining lustful and illicit desire.

The law said not to take God's name in vain. That meant, to

many, that if one took an oath—"so help me God"—he had better tell the truth. To do otherwise would be to take God's name in vain. And so it would. But what principles underlie that? One principle is that of integrity. We must be able to trust one another if we are to live together in any kind of viable society. Jesus expanded the principle. Since integrity is the desired virtue, it ought not to depend on an oath. A man's word ought to be good with or without an oath. **"Simply let your 'Yes' be 'Yes' and your 'No,' 'No' "** (v. 37). How could it be otherwise? Do we think it's OK to lie just because we haven't sworn with an oath to tell the truth?

It is clear, then, that obedience to the letter of God's Word is not enough; we must also obey its spirit or intent.

But what if obeying the spirit of the law should require us to disobey its letter? Is that conceivable? What does the Scripture itself say on the subject?

Violation of the Sabbath law was a charge specifically laid against Jesus (see John 5:16-18; Luke 13:10-17). He was also accused because His disciples allegedly violated the Sabbath. Jesus' reply in the latter case is most interesting. He does not argue that the critics have misconstrued the law, that it did not really prohibit the simple act of "harvesting" in which they were engaged. He might well have argued that, but instead he pointed to a precedent of others who *broke the letter of the law for good reason.*

"Have you never read what David did when he and his companions were hungry and in need? In the time of Abiathar the high priest, he entered the house of God and ate the consecrated bread, which is only lawful for priests to eat. And he also gave some to his companions" (Mark 2:25-26). Jesus here referred to a time when David was fleeing for his life from the unreasoning hatred of King Saul (see 1 Sam. 21). In order to get help and food from the priest at Nob, David lied about his reason for being there. The priest, suspicious that something might be wrong, had been afraid to help David, a fear that was well justified in light of the fact that when Saul learned of it he executed the whole priestly family.

Jesus does not say anything about David's lies on this occasion. He does strongly imply, however, that the violation of the law that provided for priests alone to eat of the consecrated bread (Lev. 24:9) was proper under the circumstances.

It is interesting to note that the priest who permitted David to eat the bread also apparently understood that the need of the person took precedence over the letter of the law. His primary reservation in the matter concerned not the illegality of David's eating consecrated bread but whether David was a fugitive or on legitimate business. After justifying David's and Ahimelech's breaking the letter of the law for good cause, Jesus applied the same principle to the keeping of the sacred day. **"The Sabbath was made for man, not man for the Sabbath"** (Mark 2:27).

Thus, as in His teachings considered earlier (Matt. 5:21 ff.), Jesus emphasizes the principle behind the Word. *Why* did God ordain the Sabbath? Jesus said it was not for the sake of the day, not just to have some arbitrary rule, but for *man's benefit.* If, therefore, a rigid adherence to the Sabbath rule should work out to man's detriment instead of his benefit, an exception to the rule was proper and in order. Jesus taught, in effect, that the principle or spirit of the Law was more important than the letter, that in fact they would sometimes be incompatible, and that our duty then is to obey the principle or intent of the Law.

As Jesus said to those who were stumbling over too literal an interpretation of His words, **"The Spirit gives life; the flesh counts for nothing. The words I have spoken to you are spirit and they are life"** (John 6:63).

Isn't it obvious, as we think of it, that the principles of God's Word take precedence over the letter? Suppose a father says to his son, "Go to the discount store and buy four pounds of Snyder's number 8 grass seed. It's a bit farther than the garden store, but the price is quite a bit less—$2.38 a pound as opposed to $3.29."

On the way to the discount house, the son passes the garden store and notes in the window a sign: "Half Price Sale: Snyder's number 8 grass seed—$1.65 a pound." What should the son do to obey the will of his father?

Had the father only told the son *what* to do (go to the discount house) and not told him *why* (the price is less), the son could obey the father only by going to the discount house. However, since the father told him his purpose was to get the product for less money, the son would obey his father's *will* best by stopping at the garden store, despite the father's *words* to the contrary.

The question then becomes: has God's Word only told us *what* we are to do, or has He also told us *why*. Has He given us only specific commands, or has He revealed to us the governing principles behind those commands?

Jesus said, **"In everything do to others what you would have them do to you, for *this sums up* the Law and the Prophets"** (Matt. 7:12).

Again Jesus said, **" 'Love the Lord your God with all your heart, with all your soul, and with all your mind.' This is the first and greatest commandment. And the second is like it: 'Love your neighbor as yourself.' *All the Law and the Prophets hang on these* two commandments"** (Matt. 22:37-40). Indeed the Word of God does give us the underlying principle: first, love to God, and, second, love to man.

So God's Word has told us the *why*. We are to relate to others in love.

This is not to say, as proponents of the new morality do, that love is the *only* law we need. The commandments serve important purposes; otherwise God would never have given them. For one thing, they tell us specifically what choices love will make in various areas of life. But love is the prevailing principle nevertheless, and any obedience to commands that is not an expression of love is not obedience to the spirit of God's law.

Used Rightly—A Fountain of Life

Jesus made it clear that the Word of God provides indispensable guidance for living. **" 'Man does not live on bread alone, but on every word that comes from the mouth of God,' "** He said, quoting Deuteronomy 8:3 (Matt. 4:4). Jesus quoted this Scripture in the process of resisting Satan's temptations, in which, significantly, the tempter also used the Word of God. But *Jesus used the underlying principles* while *Satan misused the words.*

Some have taken an incredibly shallow view of Jesus' use of the Word of God to defeat Satan. They have imagined that the simple expedient of quoting Scripture at Satan chases him away. To view Scripture that way is to make it practically a charm or fetish with magic powers of its own. Satan is not afraid of *words*. Jesus defeated Satan by taking the principles taught by the Word and *making those principles His standards for living.* He therefore rejected actions based on unscriptural principles ("throw yourself down" from the temple) even when Satan had plausible words from Scripture to support such actions.

If we use the Word of God as Jesus did, it will enable us to recognize and resist temptation as He did.

Jesus prayed for His followers, **"Sanctify them by the truth; your Word is truth"** (John 17:17). He said to His followers, **"You are already clean because of the word I have spoken to you"** (John 15:3). To others who were not His followers, He said, **"You are in error because you do not know the Scriptures or the power of God"** (Matt. 22:29).

So Jesus showed both sides of the coin: through the truth of God's Word we can be cleansed, but ignorance of that Word will cause us to go astray.

Subverting God's Word

It takes more than a *knowledge* of God's Word, however, for one to receive the full benefit of His Word. In His parable of the seed and the sower, Jesus described three unworthy responses to the Word of God, responses which will basically nullify its effect on one's life.

Jesus spoke first of seed that falls along the path. The birds come and eat it (Matt. 13:4). This represents a person who **"hears the message about the kingdom *and does not understand it*; the evil one comes and snatches away what was sown in his heart"** (v. 19). Jesus here once more emphasizes the necessity of understanding the Word, grasping the principles it communicates. Otherwise, the net profit from hearing the Word is zero, for Satan snatches the Word away. Actually he snatched it away at the very moment we heard it, since it did not sink down into our understanding. We could hardly retain it because we never had it.

This is a sober warning from Jesus. Rote learning or formal indoctrination in the Word when unaccompanied by the understanding imparted by the Holy Spirit (who Jesus said would teach us all things) is worthless. Actually, it can be worse than worthless because it creates an illusion of learning God's Word when no real learning has in fact occurred. Could this explain the incredible Bible ignorance of some who have been raised in the church?

The second unworthy response to the Word is pictured by the seed that **"fell on rocky places, where it did not have much soil"** (v. 5). Jesus said this represents a person **"who hears the**

**Word and at once receives it with joy. But since he has no
root, he lasts only a short time. When trouble or persecution
comes because of the Word, he quickly falls away"** (vv.
20-21).

Some people are shallow or superficial in their convictions.
They like the sound of God's Word (who wouldn't want eternal
life as a free gift?), but they do not really ponder the issues and
implications of God's Word. They make no real, deep commitment. Their Christianity is all on the surface. While they may
have some understanding of the Word as they hear it, they have
missed the most basic and profound truth of all—that Christian
faith is nothing if it does not involve a man in commitment to God
at the deepest level of his being.

Jesus spoke of yet a third unworthy response to His Word.
**"Other seed fell among thorns, which grew up and choked
the plants"** (v. 7). This represents a person who **"hears the
Word, but the worries of this life and the deceitfulness of
wealth choke it, making it unfruitful"** (v. 22).

This is perhaps the most subtle snare of all. We can fail to
benefit from the Word of God simply because we neglect it. We
allow other concerns and interests, whether good or bad in
themselves, to crowd God's Word from our minds. Not only
Jonah but all the Bible is lost to us.

We elect to live by bread alone.

The Greatest Error

The most tragic mistake any man can make in regard to the Bible
is to get only bits and pieces of truth from it while missing its
major purpose. Unfortunately, this is not only a tragic mistake but
a common one. It is all the more tragic when the person making it
honestly reveres, perhaps almost worships, the Bible as divine.

What is the great purpose of the Bible? Does it tell us how to
live—"do unto others as you'd have them do to you," and all that?
Does it tell us how to *believe*—there is one God in three Persons,
etc.? Does it give us comfort and inspiration for the hard places:
"The Lord is my Shepherd," etc.?

Indeed the Word of God does all these things and more, but we
have not yet mentioned its basic purpose. The purpose of the Bible
is to *lead people to Jesus Christ*.

"You diligently study the Scriptures because you think

that by them you possess eternal life," said Jesus (John 5:39). What did He mean, " . . . you *think* that by them you possess eternal life"?

Don't we?

No!

Jesus continued, **"These are the Scriptures that testify about Me, yet you refuse to come to Me to have life"** (John 5:39-40).

The Scriptures are a means not an end. The Bible does not save, nor was it ever intended to. You can memorize every line of it and even try to live by its matchless truths but still miss the entire point and purpose. The Bible exists to reveal Christ. If you exalt the Bible but don't know Christ, you have fallen prey to a master strategy of Satan.

Jesus said that people who trust the Bible to save them but fail to come to Him will ultimately find themselves condemned by the very Word of God in which they trusted for salvation (see John 5:45-47).

A story goes that a backwoods farmer who rarely got to town had never seen a banana. When he finally did see a stalk of bananas on an infrequent visit to a general store and heard that they were delicious fruit unlike anything he had ever tasted, he bought a bunch.

When the merchant visited the farmer a few days later to deliver some ordered goods, he saw the yard strewn with peeled bananas. "I guess you didn't like the bananas," he ventured.

"They war'nt so bad," drawled the farmer, "but they sure got a big core!"

Don't mistake the Bible for the sum and substance of God's Word while viewing Christ as a dispensable core. Christ is the whole banana, without whom the Scriptures are only peelings.

Jesus Christ undoubtedly knew the Scriptures well and loved them deeply. He quoted them frequently, showing both an intimate acquaintance with God's Word and a profound respect for it. God's Word furnished the standard by which He judged everything else, and the principles by which He Himself lived.

Nothing can profit us as Christians more than reverent study of the Word of God. With the Christ of the Word in our hearts and the Word of Christ filling our minds, we shall know what it is to truly live.

4

What Did Jesus Say About . .

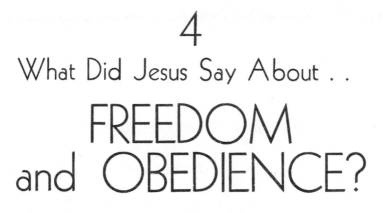

FREEDOM and OBEDIENCE?

"Love God, and do as you please."

Augustine is reputed to have said that*, but you would almost think Jesus said it the way it has been embraced and proclaimed as Christian truth.

Some Bible students think Augustine's cryptic statement well expresses the biblical love ethic. They reason: We are not under law but are called to liberty. Therefore, no rigid demands are placed upon us. More to the point, love is the fulfillment of the law. If we are truly motivated by love, we will please to do the things which God approves.

Great theory.

But does it always work?

What did Jesus say about the sufficiency of love as a control mechanism for behavior? **" 'Love the Lord your God with all your heart, with all your soul, and with all your mind.' This is the first and greatest commandment. And the second is like it: 'Love your neighbor as yourself.' All the Law and the Prophets hang on these two commandments"** (Matt. 22:37-40).

Because of these words of Jesus, Christians generally have embraced the love ethic. We believe in love as opposed to law, in

---

*Though this quotation is often attributed to Augustine, the closest thing to it seems to be "Love, and do what you like" (Augustin, *Encyclopedia of Religious Quotations,* Frank S. Mead, Revell, Old Tappan, N.J.).

liberty as good versus legalism as bad. We don't want anybody to think he *has to* do anything. We want people to love God and do as they please.

Why, then, when Christians are free to do as they please, do they so often please to do less than they ought to for Christ?

Christians sometimes don't feel like going to church, praying, reading the Bible, witnessing, giving. If they have bought the "do as you please" bit sufficiently, they just may not do those things they don't want to do. It would be a shame for them to fall into the trap of legalism! As a result, Christians have not only become increasingly free from *obligation* to behave in certain prescribed ways but some are more and more becoming free from right behavior.

The effect of this is a languishing and powerless church. Meanwhile "legalists" aggressively advance. They dominate their people. "It's your business to get out there and witness; to go, give, and pray, and read your Bible every day." And the people do it.

Where Are We Going Wrong?

If only Augustine taught it, we'd decide his statement confers too much freedom. But what are we going to do with the teachings of Jesus? He's the One who said love comprehends and fulfills all the demands of the law. Isn't that the same thing Augustine says?

No, it is not.

The problem is that we have made a subtle shift without even knowing it. We think: *love over law,* but we act out *feelings over faith.* And the confusion is partly Augustine's fault.

It may sound as if there is little or no difference between his teaching and that of Jesus. But an entirely different—and destructive—dynamic comes into operation.

The whole issue turns on that little phrase: *do as you please.* Through that expression *feelings* infiltrate where they have no right. We have equated *do as you please* with *do whatever you feel like doing.* And no wonder, for if there's a difference, it hasn't been distinguished.

Take prayer. Since I am still in the flesh, the idea of praying doesn't always please me. Jesus said to His disciples in Gethsemane, **"Watch and pray so that you will not fall into temptation. The spirit is willing, but the body is weak"** (Mark 14:38). My mind, however, listening to Augustine here instead of

Jesus, can easily follow the track: Since I don't want to pray, if I did so it would be a legalistic thing and therefore wrongly motivated and unacceptable.

Or take cheerfulness and confidence. Jesus said, **"Do not let your hearts be troubled and do not be afraid. In this world you will have trouble. But take heart! I have overcome the world"** (John 14:27; 16:33). Not always remembering His assurances, I sometimes feel discouraged, troubled, unhappy. I don't feel like smiling or taking heart. Surely if I smile when I don't feel like it, I will be guilty of hypocrisy. Won't I?

What about attending church? Jesus' custom was to go to the synagogue every Sabbath, and the Bible tells me that, as a Christian, I should not forsake the assembling with other believers (Heb. 10:25). But what if I don't want to go to church? What if I don't happen to feel like going? Wouldn't my participation be meaningless? Even a mockery?

And what if I don't want to give? If I really can't see my way clear to make significant contributions, if such liberality is not unhesitating and purely in line with my desires, it would be unacceptable to Him who loves a cheerful giver. Wouldn't it?

The above examples describe the way we often think. These are projections of the Augustinian principle: love God and do as you please . . . which we have practically applied as love God but don't think you have to do your *duty* (ugly legalistic word!) if you don't feel like doing it.

Would it indeed be legalism if I prayed, smiled, worshiped, and gave contrary to my natural inclination of the moment? Certainly not. It would be the *obedience of faith.*

Over against Augustine's "do as you please," we need to consider the Lord Jesus Christ's words: **"If you love Me, you will do what I command"** (John 14:15).

When Jesus speaks of love here, He is talking about the *why,* the motive for our behavior. It must be love. But love is not altogether or even primarily a feeling. Psychiatrist James D. Mallory defines love as a volitional attitude, a stance taken by an act of the will:

"The tendency to think of love as some strong feeling which compels one to behave in a certain way is very common . . . It seems to be so much easier to behave a certain way if one has a compelling feeling. Of course, any animal behaves on that frequency. There is nothing distinctively human and certainly nothing Christian about responding to a strong feeling, a motivation.

"A crucial aspect of love is its volitional element. Love involves an act of the will, a choice, a commitment. The true characteristics of love are set forth in what is generally acknowledged to be one of the greatest passages of prose in the English language, 1 Corinthians 13. . . . Notice that this beautiful passage describing love says nothing about feelings or emotions. Every single quality attributed to love is an attitude that we may have toward someone with an act of our wills that are turned over to God" (*The Kink and I—a Psychiatrist's Guide to Untwisted Living,* Victor Books, Wheaton, Ill.).

As you consider this definition of love, Augustine's statement becomes all the less valid. It is not only joining two things that don't go together (love and doing as you please, grapes and thistles), but it is joining things that are in hostile tension.

Love is by definition a commitment to another person. It involves a specific choice *not* to do as you please but to do what pleases the one loved.

This is true of married love. "A married man is concerned about the affairs of this world—*how he can please his wife*" (1 Cor. 7:33; see also v. 34).

It is true of the Christian ministry. "Even as I try to *please everybody* in every way. For I am *not seeking my own good but the good of many,* so that they may be saved" (1 Cor. 10:33).

It is true of Christian love for our brethren. "We who are strong ought to bear with the failings of the weak, and *not to please ourselves.* Each of us should *please his neighbor* for his good, to build him up. For even *Christ* did not please Himself" (Rom. 15:1-3).

Love God and do as you please? That is self-contradictory. It would be more accurate to say: Love God *or* do as you please; it cannot be both. Why, even the sinless Christ did not find the things that naturally pleased Him as a man to be consistent with His love for God and for others. He had to choose. He chose to "not please Himself." That is why He prayed in the agony of Gethsemane, **"Yet not as I will, but as You will"** (Matt. 26:39).

There is tension between what we please to do and what we ought to do, however spiritual we may be. Jesus experienced that tension in the Garden. No other interpretation of His prayer makes sense. Had Jesus loved God and done as He [Jesus] pleased, there would have been no cross for Him and no salvation for us.

And if we do as we please, there will be no cross for us . . . and no resultant blessing for those we were meant to serve.

Jesus said, **"If you love Me, you will do what I command"** (John 14:15). "Love" is the *why*; "do what I command" is the *what*. This is the obedience of faith.

How would it have worked for the great men of faith of all ages to have loved God and done as they pleased? How would it have worked for Abraham when he was told, "Take now thy son, thine only son Isaac, whom thou lovest, and get thee into the land of Moriah, and offer him there for a burnt offering"? (Gen. 22:2, KJV) Scripture tells us it was "by faith Abraham, when God tested him, offered Isaac as a sacrifice" (Heb. 11:17). The obedience of faith will sustain us when loving God and doing as we please would let us utterly fail.

Does it seem that the obedience of faith does away with our freedom? Not so. "You, my brothers, were called to be free. But do not use your freedom to indulge your sinful nature [to do what you please!]; rather, serve one another in love" (Gal. 5:13).

The Fruits of Obedience
What would happen if Christians generally were to begin obeying the One whom they say they love?

We don't have to guess at an answer to that question. Jesus has told us what would happen. **"If you obey My commands, you will remain in My love, just as I have obeyed My Father's commands and remain in His love"** (John 15:10).

There is a teaching abroad in the land that sometimes causes people to dismiss these words of Jesus lightly. That is the teaching that God's love is changeless and unconditional, that He loves us just the same regardless of who we are or what we do. If one holds that view, there is no moral force whatever in these words of Jesus. Why should I be concerned about obeying Jesus' commands in order to abide in His love if my place in His love is unassailable and changeless?

The saying that Jesus "loves us just the same regardless of what we do," that His love is unconditional, is, like Augustine's saying, only true in a special and limited sense. The key words here are *just the same.* It is true that God loves men even while they are unrepentant sinners (Rom. 5:6-8). It is true that God loves His own even when we are out of fellowship with Him, as the father loved the wandering prodigal (Luke 15:11-32).

It is not true, however, that He loves us *just the same* when we are living in disobedience to Him. And we might well question whether it is true that He loves all of His followers equally, without distinction. We hear this repeated by multitudes of Christians, but will it stand scrutiny according to the teachings of Jesus?

We may say He loves everyone the same, but *He* says, **"If you obey My commands, you will remain in My love."** The obvious implication is that if we do not obey His commands, we will not remain in His love in the same way we would otherwise. In the face of this, can we still claim He will love us just as much and in the same way if we generally resist Him as if we generally obeyed Him? To do so would seem to strip language of its meaning.

The Scripture calls the Apostle John the disciple whom Jesus loved (John 19:26-27; 20:2; 21:7, 20). What does that mean? If Jesus loved all the disciples equally, it doesn't mean anything. Jesus no doubt loved John in a special way. Could that have anything to do with the fact that John's devotion to Him was such that John alone followed the Master into the bitterest hour of his trial before Pilate? And stood with Him even at the cross, when all the rest had forsaken Him and fled?

Parents ordinarily love all their children, but they do not love them all the same. A thoughtful, loving, obedient child often has a special place in a parent's heart. And why not?

Jude must not have thought the Lord loved everybody the same regardless of whether they lived in obedience or not. He wrote to Christians, "Keep yourselves in God's love as you wait for the mercy of our Lord Jesus Christ to bring you to eternal life" (Jude 21).

It is meaningless for Jude to tell us to keep ourselves in God's love if there is no way we can in any sense fall out of God's love! The fact is that Jesus has promised special favor to those who, instead of doing as they please, will choose to obey God whether they feel like it or not because they have made a love commitment to Him. Such people will "remain in My love."

The word here translated *remain* is *abide* in the King James

Version. It has the idea of God's love resting on a person—of a settled, continual focusing of His love. To be the object of that kind of love is about the most wonderful thing imaginable. To have *anyone* focus loving attention on us is to be extremely privileged. But to be the object of *God's* love . . . what could be better?

Jesus told His disciples something of what it would mean to them to remain in His love. It would mean answered prayer (John 15:7) and it would mean enriched love among the brethren (v. 12). All in all, it would mean full joy in the Christian life (v. 11).

What would we think if our prayers began to be answered as never before, if our personal relations with other Christians became as warm and fulfilling regularly as they have been at some high points along the way, if a deep and abiding joy accompanied us everywhere? We might well think that personal revival had come to us.

And we would be right. But these are the benefits Jesus offers to those who love Him and keep His commandments. Obedience, when prompted by love, brings revival. Indeed, obedience prompted by love *is* revival. This is a revival you can have . . . now.

5
What Did Jesus Say About . . .
HIMSELF?

Remember Cassius Clay? You know, "I'm the greatest." He is better known now as Muhammed Ali. He seems to think he's the greatest fighter who ever lived, and if you want to know about it, just ask him and he'd be glad to tell you.

Evel Knievel perhaps thinks he's the greatest motorcyclist who ever got on the wheels. Henry Kissinger may feel he's the world's foremost diplomat. Some people claim to be the greatest in their particular field of endeavor.

Others make even more exalted claims. They think they are the greatest people living, period. You'll find some such people in mental institutions. They suffer from what's called delusions of grandeur. Maybe one will have a three-cornered hat on, and a hand in his jacket. He thinks he's Napoleon.

But all those who think they are the greatest in their field, and even those who imagine they are the greatest men on earth, fall short in their claims as compared with Jesus. Actually, He claimed to be God!

If that man in the institution thinks he's Napoleon, and you can tell it by what he says and by the way he acts and dresses, I say that Jesus Christ thought He was God, and you can tell it by what He said and the way He acted! If we fail to examine Jesus' claims seriously, we just haven't yet faced up to the question of His identity. There are those who insist with good reason that you have to put Jesus down as a lunatic, a liar, or the Lord. He was one of the three.

Jesus will not permit us to take a different view and say, "Well, He was a great religious teacher. Of course He was not the Son of God, and he was not the Lord of heaven, but He was a very enlightened, advanced man." He will not allow us to take that position because, you see, He represented Himself to be much more than an enlightened teacher. He claimed to be the Lord of heaven. And either he was the Lord of heaven, or that was a false assertion. And if it was a false assertion, then either He lied or He was demented. If you really come to grips with the facts of the case, you have to conclude that Jesus was indeed a lunatic, a liar, or the Lord.

No Less Than God

Let's consider some of Jesus' claims. Those who were contemporaries of Jesus understood very well, better than many people do today, what Jesus' claims were. That's why they crucified Him! They charged Him with blasphemy because of His "ridiculous," exalted, outrageous assertion that He, a mere man, the son of Joseph the carpenter, *was God.* In John 10:31-33 we can read about the reactions of the people to Jesus. "Again the Jews picked up stones to stone Him, but Jesus said to them, **'I have shown you many great miracles from the Father. For which of these do you stone Me?'**

" 'We are not stoning you for any of these,' replied the Jews, 'but for blasphemy, because you, a mere man, claim to be God.' "

Jesus had performed many works of mercy and compassion. He had healed people. He had helped the downtrodden. He had delivered the demon possessed. He asked for which of these they hated Him and wanted to kill Him.

They said, "No, no, not for Your works! Not for what You do, but for what You *say,* for blasphemy, because You make Yourself God." They thought Jesus was claiming to be on a par with God, and they were right!

Now, what made the Jews think that Jesus claimed equality with God? Many things. It starts at the beginning of Jesus' ministry. Remember when they brought a man sick of the palsy to Jesus? They carried him on his bed, and had to come down through the roof to get him before Jesus, because the crowd was so great they could not come near the Lord otherwise. "When Jesus saw their faith, He said to the paralytic, **'Son, your sins are forgiven.'**

Now some teachers of the law were sitting there, thinking to themselves, 'Why does this fellow talk like that? He's blaspheming! Who can forgive sins but God alone?' " (Mark 2:5-7)

They inwardly accused Jesus of usurping divine prerogatives because He claimed He could forgive sins. He said to this man, **"Your sins are forgiven."** And the people standing around thought, *That's a terrible thing for Him to say. Who does He think He is? Nobody has the power to forgive sins except God.* And they were right. Jesus was claiming to be God when He stated, **"Your sins are forgiven."**

The passage continues, "Jesus knew in His spirit that this was what they were thinking in their hearts, and He said to them, **'Why are you thinking these things? Which is easier: to say to the paralytic, "Your sins are forgiven," or to say, "Get up, take your mat and walk"? But that you may know that the Son of man has authority on earth to forgive sins . . . , He said to the paralytic, 'I tell you, get up, take your mat and go home.'** He got up, took his mat, and walked out in full view of them all" (Mark 2:8-12).

Now, you see, Jesus says in effect, "If I say to this man, 'Your sins be forgiven,' you people watching have no way of knowing whether I have power to forgive his sins or not. You can't see whether his sins are forgiven. But which is easier? To say, 'Your sins are forgiven,' or, 'Take up your bed and walk.' " Only God could make *either* statement operative. So Jesus healed the man as a demonstration of His divine power, as an evidence of His ability both to heal, which they could see, and to forgive, which they could not see.

Jesus claimed not only divine power to forgive sin and heal but also the right to receive worship **"Ye call Me Master and Lord, and ye say well; for so I am"** (John 13:13, KJV). Jesus did not refuse worship; He accepted it as His right.

It is the worst form of blasphemy to accept worship if you're not God. For you or for me to accept worship would be outrageous, unthinkable. There was one man, named Herod, who did that very thing. He gave a speech, and the people, in order to butter him up, said, "Oh, the voice of a god, and not of a man." Herod thought that was pretty nice praise, but God struck him down. He was eaten by worms and died, because he took God's glory. But Jesus said, **"You call Me Master and Lord, rightly**

so, because I am." Now those are stiff claims, outrageous claims, if indeed He is not what He claimed.

Jesus also taught that He had power over life and death, even His own. **"Therefore does My Father love Me, because I lay down My life, that I might take it again. No man taketh it from Me, but I lay it down of Myself. I have power to lay it down, and I have power to take it again"** (John 10:17-18, KJV).

Nobody can make such a claim, humanly speaking. You couldn't claim that. I couldn't. I could lay down my life, I suppose, if I wanted to commit suicide. I certainly could not say that no man has power to take my life from me, as Jesus did. And if I did lay down my life, I certainly could not say, "And I have power to take it again," that is, to reclaim life once I was dead. Jesus said He could do that, and then he proved it by doing it, as we celebrate every Easter.

Jesus Christ said He not only had power over His own life, but also had power to give life to other people. Again only God can impart life, but Jesus said He could do it. **"For just as the Father raises the dead and gives them life, even so the Son gives life to whom He is pleased to give it"** (John 5:21).

Jesus' stupendous claims also included having the power of ultimate judgment over the human race. He said that men would stand before Him to give account for their lives and their deeds. **"For the Father judgeth no man, but hath committed all judgment unto the Son"** (John 5:22). Obviously, that's a claim to deity. Final judgment is a function that belongs to God.

Jesus capped His tremendous claims by stating flatly that men should **"honor the Son, even as they honor the Father"** (John 5:23). This is what distinguishes the Christian from the cultist or from the adherent of some other religion. The Christian ranks Jesus Christ with God Himself. And he does so because Jesus taught him to do it. Others may "honor" Jesus as a prophet (as Muslims do) or as a god (small *g*, as Jehovah's Witnesses do) or as a great man (as almost anyone may do), but it is hardly an *honor* to One equal with God to call Him a great guy!

We have by no means exhausted the biblical passages relating to Jesus' various claims to deity. For example, Jesus also claimed He had power to give everlasting life. **"The Son gives life to whom He is pleased to give it"** (John 5:21). **"Whoever hears**

My word and believes Him who sent Me has eternal life"
(John 5:24).

Jesus claimed He had power to order the angels of heaven to
action. **"They** [men] **will see the Son of Man coming on the
clouds of the sky, with power and great glory. And He will
send His angels with a loud trumpet call, and they will
gather His elect from the four winds, from one end of the
heavens to the other"** (Matt. 24:30-31).

Jesus' claims to deity can be summed up in no better words than
His own, as recorded at the close of the Gospel of Matthew. **"All
authority in heaven and on earth has been given to Me"**
(28:18). That is about as big and strong and broad a claim as a
man could possibly make—absolute dominion, both on earth and
in heaven.

You hear about people who exercise great authority. You read
a story of a great plantation owner. He has 6,000 acres, and he
goes outside and stands on his veranda and looks over it—he's
master of all he surveys. What a sense of power!

Something similar may happen to a kid with his first bike or a
man with his first car. He has a sense of ownership and power,
especially if he has it paid for! Even if he hasn't, he may think he's
big stuff. "All authority is given unto me over this brand new
Vega. WOW!" This is how people often react. We have our
possessions, and they give us a certain sense of authority or power.
We like power.

Jesus says that His relationship to the whole earth and heaven
is like that. He has power over it all. He is Master of all He
surveys.

We are not wide of the mark, then, when we say that Jesus
made absolutely the most exalted claims any human being ever
made or possibly could make. And those are indeed outrageous
claims if they are not true. His contemporaries, at least those in
authority, said that they were not true, and that such a man did
not deserve to live. They were more consistent than many people
today who take a neutral, indifferent attitude toward Jesus. The
contemporaries of Jesus at least took His claims seriously, but
they rejected them. So He had to die for blasphemy.

You need to decide whether Jesus Christ is indeed a blasphemer.
Is He a lunatic, a liar, or the Lord? It makes all the difference in
the world. If He is telling the truth, the implications are impossible

to exaggerate. If He really is our Judge, and we're going to meet Him someday, if He alone does have power to give us life—we can't afford to ignore Him. So you have to decide.

A Real Flesh-and-Blood Man

Jesus had a few other things to say about Himself that we must not overlook, because He not only made exalted claims to deity, but He also fully endorsed His own humanity and his limitations. With all our proper emphasis on Jesus being divine—God come in the flesh—people sometimes get the idea that He wasn't human, that He wasn't a true man. They imagine He was a phantom of some kind, that He was God in disguise, God masquerading as a human being.

That is not the case. He was God. He claimed all the powers of God, but He was also a true man.

Jesus' favorite name for Himself was Son of man. He was also called the Son of God, but more often, especially as recorded by Luke, He speaks of Himself as the Son of man. He was always God, but He became a man when He was born of Mary. That was a very special and important thing to Him.

How can one be both God and man? I don't understand it. I don't demand that I should understand it. It is greater than my mind. I don't expect to fully exhaust the identity and reality that is God. But the Bible clearly teaches both the humanity and deity of Christ. This is so important. People try to bring God down to their level and explain Him totally, and if something doesn't fit, they make it fit. And they do violence to the Word of God. Our business is to make our doctrines fit the Word of God, not vice versa.

Jesus said, **"I tell you the truth, the Son can do nothing by Himself. . . ."** Does that sound like the same man speaking who said, **"All authority in heaven and on earth has been given to Me"**? His statements are certainly paradoxical, but they are not contradictory. Our task is to honor all that the Scripture says. Jesus said, **"The Son can do nothing by Himself; He can do only what He sees His father doing, because whatever the Father does, the Son also does"** (John 5:19). Again, Jesus said, **"By Myself I can do nothing; I judge only as I hear, and My judgment is just, for I seek not to please Myself but Him who sent Me"** (John 5:30).

Jesus said that He didn't even know when He was going to return. **"No one knows about that day or hour, not even the angels in heaven, nor the Son, but only the Father"** (Mark 13:32). One of the attributes of God is to know everything. Yet Jesus Christ in His humanity did not know the hour of His return, because He was true man.

Furthermore, and this is probably the most important of all, Jesus Christ, as a human being, submitted His will to God the Father; He did not insist on doing His own will. Now that is the nature of God—to do His own will. He's sovereign. Who can say to God, "What are You doing?" Who can say anything in the way of question or rebuke? God does whatever He wants to do because He's God.

Jesus is God, but He doesn't do whatever He wants to do, because He's also a man. A man's place is to obey God, to be subject to Him. So, Jesus said, **"My food is to do the will of Him who sent Me and to finish His work"** (John 4:34). In the garden of Gethsemane, Jesus prayed, **"Not My will, but Yours be done"** (Luke 22:42). When He said that, Jesus was taking the position of a creature, of a subject, of a man.

Yes, Jesus claimed to possess all the prerogatives of God, but He also said that He was a human being with all the nature of a human being.

The *Sine Qua Non* of Life

I hate for people to lay foreign phrases on me, so I don't do it very often to others, but I'm going to do it now. Jesus claimed to be both the all sufficient Saviour and the *sine qua non* of life. That is a good phrase: *sine qua non.* I took Latin, and I don't know much of it, but *sine qua non* literally means *without which not,* or *without which, nothing.* Webster defines it as "an absolutely indispensable or essential thing." Jesus claimed that He is the *sine qua non,* that without Him, we are nothing; everything is lost. He is the essential to life.

But He is also *enough* to give life; He is the Saviour. That is, if you do have Him, you have everything you need! Not easy answers. Not automatic solutions to every problem. But in Christ you are complete (Col. 2:10). You have the capacity, the potential for all that life should be. You can become all that God intended in order to fulfill your destiny.

Many of the blessings we have by virtue of our relationship to Christ are suggested by the great "I am's" of the Gospel of John. These "I am's" reveal how Jesus is both the *sine qua non* and the all sufficient Saviour. For instance, Jesus said of Himself, **"I am the bread of life"** (John 6:35). Without Him, we are unfed, spiritually. With Him, we are sufficed and nourished.

Jesus said, **"I am the light of the world"** (John 8:12). Without Him, we are in total darkness, spiritually. We don't know where we are going. We are the blind leading the blind. With Him, we have light. We do not walk in darkness. We know which way to go and what decisions to make. Jesus said, **"I am the light of the world. Whoever follows Me will never walk in darkness, but will have the light of life"** (John 8:12).

Jesus said **"I am the good shepherd"** (John 10:11), and without Him we stray as sheep without a shepherd, wandering, stumbling through life, uncared for, unguided. With Him we have that tender care we read about in the Scripture: the shepherd will even give His life for the sheep (John 10:11).

Jesus said, **"I am the resurrection and the life"** (John 11:25). Without Him, even our living is slow dying. With Him, even our dying is but an incidental interlude in our eternal living. **"He who believes in Me will live, even though he dies; and whoever lives and believes in Me will never die"** (John 11:25-26).

Jesus said, **"I am the vine"** (John 15:5). Without Him, our lives can only be unfruitful because we are like branches cut off from the vine. The vital source of life is Christ; this life must come to us through Him. And with Him, we can bear lasting fruit (see John 15:16).

Underlying all the other "I am's" of Jesus is His claim recorded in John 8: **"Your father Abraham rejoiced at the thought of seeing My day; he saw it and was glad."**

"You are not yet 50 years old," the Jews said to Him, "and You have seen Abraham?"

"I tell you the truth," Jesus answered, **"before Abraham was born, *I am!*"** (vv. 56-58)

Jesus could say, "I am . . ." (all the various things He claimed) because He is the I AM, the self-existent, eternal God. The Jews very well understood Him to be making that claim, for "at this, they picked up stones to stone Him" for blasphemy (v. 59).

Because He is the *sine qua non* of life and the all sufficient Saviour, Jesus gave a great invitation. He said, **"Come to Me, all you who are weary and burdened, and I will give you rest"** (Matt. 11:28). Note that He did not say come to the church, be a good guy, keep the Ten Commandments, keep the Golden Rule, or a thousand other things. He said, **"Come to Me all you who are weary and burdened."** What human being has not been burdened with the load of his humanity? Who hasn't labored against his own baser instincts, against his sins and temptations, against the misunderstanding of other people. **"Come to Me,"** Jesus says, **"and I will give you rest."**

When Jesus says, **"I will give you rest,"** He is claiming to be the sufficient answer to your needs. Because you can't really rest until your problem is resolved. The Bible compares man to "the troubled sea, when it cannot rest, whose waters cast up mire and dirt" (Isa. 57:20). This is a graphic description of the constant turmoil which characterizes many people's lives. Maybe they can find escape briefly. Maybe they can sleep with sleeping pills—or even without them—but they don't have real rest until these problems are resolved. That's what Jesus offers to do for you— give you rest. And that suggests a resolution of your problems. Not that they all disappear, but in fact you have entered into the presence of the Lord, who is bigger than any problem. He has all power.

But even more critical than your need for rest, as crucial as that is, Jesus claimed that your response to Him and His teaching will *absolutely determine the success or failure of your life*. Not the *apparent* success or failure, but the absolute, the real success or failure of your life.

"Therefore, everyone who hears these words of Mine and puts them into practice is like a wise man who built his house on the rock. The rain came down, the streams rose, and the winds blew and beat against that house; yet it did not fall, because it had its foundation on the rock. But everyone who hears these words of Mine and does not put them into practice is like a foolish man who built his house on sand. The rain came down, the streams rose, and the winds blew and beat against that house, and it fell with a great crash" (Matt. 7:24-27).

You can build the "house" of your life without Jesus Christ, and without His sayings. You may even build a great house without Him, but the final result will simply be a great fall. The bigger you build, the bigger the collapse and the bigger the ruins.

Witness Watergate.

Your house built without Christ may fall in this life, and very likely will; but if not, it will certainly fall in the coming storm of death and judgment. According to Jesus, to build apart from Him is just the same as building on sand. And *sine qua non*—without Him it will be nothing. The end, the net result will be zero. But with Him—the all sufficient Saviour—that house will stand, because it's founded on a rock.

6
What Did Jesus Say About . . .
GOD?

- To the pantheist, God is nature and nature is God.
- To the neoorthodox, God is the unknowable "ground of all being."
- To the Mormon, God has a body and is practically an exalted man.
- To the logical positivist, all talk of God is nonsense.
- To the Ameri-Christian posi-thinker, God is a nice old man in the sky (white, Anglo-Saxon, Protestant, of course!).
- To the behaviorist, God is a myth.
- To the communist, "God" is an enemy of the people.
- To the deist, God is an "absentee landlord" or first cause.
- To Jesus—well, Jesus said some very important things about God. From His words a rather detailed description can be drawn, revealing how near, or more often, how far from the truth other concepts are.

Perhaps the most direct description of God to come from the lips of Jesus is: **"God is spirit, and His worshipers must worship in spirit and in truth"** (John 4:24).

These words of Jesus immediately reveal the error of Mormons and all others who picture an anthropomorphic (man-like) God. God is spirit, and as Jesus said on another occasion, **"A spirit hath not flesh and bones"** (Luke 24:39, KJV). The Greek word translated *spirit* in these two passages is identical, and Jesus was clearly teaching that God is not a glorified man. In fact He has no body of any kind.

This teaching has often been disputed. Some have cited passages in the Old Testament that describe the bodily parts of God. Isaiah wrote, "Behold, the Lord's *hand* is not shortened, that it cannot save; neither His *ear* heavy, that it cannot hear, but . . . your sins have hid His *face* from you" (59:1-2). Other passages mention God's eyes (2 Chron. 16:9), His fingers (Ps. 8:3), and His mouth (Isa. 1:20). "If God has all those parts, it seems rather obvious that He has a body," some say.

But these references to body parts are no doubt examples of language accommodation; they describe God's activities in terms of the bodily members that we usually associate with them. They only mean that God sees, hears, speaks, and so forth. Were one to insist that these terms literally describe God's body, he would have real difficulty with passages such as Ruth 2:12: "A full reward be given thee of the Lord God of Israel, under whose *wings* thou art come to trust." As Walter Martin has said, If *that* is literal, God must be a chicken! (See also Pss. 36:7; 57:1; 61:4, 91:4.)

Jesus not only taught that God is spirit, but He indicated that understanding that truth is essential to proper worship. Since God is spirit, we must worship Him in spirit. Materialistic or physical or formal worship unaccompanied by genuine spiritual exercise of soul will not do.

In a few words, Jesus revealed a great deal about God. Not only God's spiritual nature but His personality and His relatedness to man are established in the one brief statement: **"True worshipers will worship the Father in spirit and in truth, for they are the kind of worshipers the Father seeks. God is spirit"** (John 4:23-24).

Far from being an impersonal "ground of being" or a primal force of some kind, God is a Person who actively relates to human beings. He is not just Mother Nature by another name. God seeks enlightened worshipers.

Yet, though God is a Person, He is not just like us. He is a sovereign and omnipotent spirit. He *can be* known and worshiped because He is a person. He *should be* worshiped because He is more than just a person; He is the unique and only true and living God. Jesus described God's supremacy with such statements as, **"With man this is impossible, but with God all things are possible"** (Matt. 19:26), and **"My Father . . . is greater than all"** (John 10:29).

He told Pilate, the Roman governor who sentenced Him to crucifixion, **"You have no power over Me that was not given to you from above"** (John 19:11). No earthly ruler is outside of God's jurisdiction. He gives and takes away thrones and kingdoms. If we defer to rulers, how much more ought we defer to the ruler's Ruler?

He Is Holy and All-knowing

Jesus told His disciples, **"Your heavenly Father is perfect"** (Matt. 5:48). God's perfection applies to every aspect of His being. If this were not true, He would not be perfect, for the word means "being entirely without fault or defect, flawless." It is a word that admits no comparison. That is, some cannot be perfect while others are more perfect and still others most perfect. Since perfect is flawless, there is no such thing as being more perfect.

Thus Jesus addressed God as **"Holy Father"** (John 17:11). God is perfect in His holiness, entirely apart from moral defect.

Jesus also taught that God knows everything perfectly, including our secret sins and inmost thoughts. God's holiness and His omniscience taken together form a devastating combination. He knows—and burns in holy indigation against—our sins.

Ever since sin entered human experience, man has been engaged in a futile cover-up. Adam and Eve tried to cover their nakedness with fig leaves (Gen. 3:7), and then tried to hide from God among the trees of the garden (Gen. 3:8).

Richard Nixon tried to cover up his knowledge of White House involvement in the Watergate affair, using one desperate measure after another to avoid disclosing his secret. But in Richard Nixon's case, his wrongdoing was electronically recorded. When the Supreme Court ruled that he had to turn over his tapes to investigators, his doom was sealed.

Jesus taught that we all stand in similar jeopardy before God. He knows what we've been up to! Not only does He know about our misdeeds, but He is going to make the evidence public. Jesus said, **"There is nothing concealed that will not be disclosed, or hidden that will not be made known. What you have said in the dark will be heard in the daylight, and what you have whispered in the ear behind closed doors will be proclaimed from the housetops"** (Luke 12:2-3).

What a frightening prospect! Unfaithful spouses, disobedient children, dishonest employees—and *all the rest of us*—have guilty secrets. And *God knows* them! Jesus said, **"You are the ones who justify yourselves in the eyes of men, but God knows your hearts"** (Luke 16:15).

He Is a God of Love

Because He does know about our sins, and because He is holy, God cannot possibly ignore our sins. But *He can forgive them.*

Jesus taught that God is a loving God, who desires to arrange a pardon for us. He said, **"For God so loved the world that He gave His only begotten Son, that whosoever believeth in Him should not perish but have everlasting life. For God sent not His Son into the world to condemn the world but that the world through Him might be saved"** (John 3:16-17, KJV).

Jesus illustrated the depth of God's love for sinful men with His parable of the lost sheep, the lost coin, and the lost son (Luke 15:3-32). For love of one lost sheep the shepherd leaves the flock and searches until he finds it and comes home rejoicing. For the sake of one lost coin out of 10, a woman diligently sweeps the house, and excitedly shares the good news with her neighbors when her search proves successful. And when an errant son returns home, the father proclaims a celebration, receiving the former rebel with great joy.

Just so, God is more than willing to pardon our sins. He so eagerly desires to forgive us that He provided an atonement at great cost to Himself—the sacrifice of His Son. And when we repent, He proclaims a celebration in heaven!

However, if we spurn or neglect the pardon offered to us through Christ, God's holiness requires that we pay the penalty of our sin. Jesus said, **"He that believeth on Him** [God's Son, Jesus] **is not condemned, but he that believeth not is condemned already, because he hath not believed in the name of the only begotten Son of God"** (John 3:18, KJV).

Nevertheless, His provision of salvation proves beyond all doubt the reality and depth of His love.

He is Kind and Benevolent

The love God showed in providing salvation is in perfect keeping with His kind and benevolent nature. Jesus taught that God is good, so uniquely good, in fact, that by comparison to God no one else even deserves to be described by that word (see Matt. 19:17). This is true whether we understand *good* to refer to His moral character or to His benevolence.

God's goodness is such that He gives to man simply out of the kindness of His own being. God pours out His bounty even upon men who are in rebellion against Him, men conspicuously unworthy to receive any divine benefits. Jesus said, **"He causes His sun to rise on the evil and the good, and sends rain on the righteous and the unrighteous"** (Matt. 5:45).

However, God particularly delights to give good gifts to those who love Him.

The favorite name Jesus used for God is significant in this connection. He called Him *Father*. Of course, Jesus had a unique right to call God His Father, because Jesus is the "only begotten Son of God" (John 3:16, and see chap. 5). But Jesus referred to God not only as "My Father" but as "the Father" and "your Father."

This marks a striking departure from the Old Testament. God is seldom called Father in the Old Testament. But the Bible says that through faith in Christ we can be born into God's family: "To all who received Him, to those who believed in His name, He gave the right *to become children of God"* (John 1:12).

So Jesus taught that we not only can be true worshipers of God, but, amazing as it is, we can be His true children.

Many indeed arrogate this privilege to themselves without receiving Christ. They assume that all men are children of God, not recognizing that nobody knew God as Father until Jesus came, and even since, becoming a child of God depends on receiving Christ.

Nevertheless, the name itself speaks volumes about the benevolent nature of God. All the warm associations of the word *father,* taken in its best human aspects, relate to Him. Jesus compared earthly fathers with God as follows: **"Which of you, if his son asks for bread, will give him a stone? Or if he asks for a fish, will he give him a snake? If you, then, though you are evil, know how to give good gifts to your children, how much more will your Father in heaven give good gifts to those who ask Him!"** (Matt. 7:9-11)

God's benevolence closely relates to His omniscience. Just as His holiness taken together with His knowledge is devastating to the sinner, so His kindness combined with His knowledge assures a wonderful providential care for His children.

Jesus said that God observes those who give in secret, hears those who pray in secret, and sees those who fast in secret, to reward each openly (Matt. 6:4, 6, 18). He also said, **"Your Father knows what you need before you ask Him"** (Matt. 6:8).

Thus we see that God does not simply know about His creatures in a detached way, as a celestial Observer amusing Himself with the unfolding drama of life on earth. Instead, He actively relates to the affairs of His people, even in small details.

Some think that a God who created the universe is much too great to be concerned with mere man, who is, to the objective mind of the scientist, a minute organism on an insignificant planet in one of the lesser solar systems of an incredibly immense universe. They make the error of associating God's greatness with man's. Since a great man only does "important" tasks and delegates lesser duties to lesser people, they think a Being as great as God surely would not occupy Himself with our trivial concerns.

Jesus firmly contradicted such a view of God. His greatness is such that He can uphold the whirling planets and stars in their orbits and concern Himself with the hurt of an orphan at the same time. Jesus said, **"See that you do not look down on one of these little ones** [children]. **For I tell you that their angels in heaven always see the face of My Father in heaven"** (Matt. 18:10). The implication seems to be that God so loves children that He has appointed a guardian angel to each one. And these angels have priority status in the court of heaven. They have instant access to the throne of God.

The world would no doubt be a better place if earth's "greats" would take a lesson from God and not be so concerned with important projects that they have no time for little people. Julia Ward Howe, who wrote "The Battle Hymn of the Republic," once interceded for a citizen with his congressman in Washington, D.C. The congressman was "too busy with important affairs of state" to consider the citizen's case. "We may be thankful that, according to the last notice," observed Julia Ward Howe, "*God* has not yet gotten that high!"

She was right. Jesus said, **"Are not two sparrows sold for a penny? Yet not one of them will fall to the ground apart**

from the will of your Father. And even the very hairs of your head are all numbered. So don't be afraid; you are worth more than many sparrows" (Matt. 10:29-31).

Certainly, if God troubles Himself with sparrows and with how many hairs we have on our heads, no concern of ours is too small to come before Him.

This does not mean, of course, that nothing bad can happen to us. Sparrows do fall. Humans do suffer, even the most godly of them. To think otherwise is to open oneself to disillusionment.

One pastor fell into this error. When his son was killed in battle, his anger at God moved him very close to sacrilege. "Where was God when my son was killed," he asked bitterly, *"watching sparrows?"*

"God was in the same place when your son was killed," came the reply, "as He was when His Son was killed!" God allowed the crucifixion, but out of it He brought salvation and the richest blessings mankind has known. God may allow affliction and tragedy to come to us, but He will bring good from it if we trust Him (Rom. 8:28-29).

God knows. God *cares*. What a solace in sorrow!

Putting It All Together

From all that Jesus said, a clear picture of God emerges. He is an "other" who seeks to relate to us. Though He is the almighty, holy, perfect, all-knowing, eternal Spirit, He loves sinful man and sent Christ to reconcile us to Himself. When we receive Christ, God becomes our Father, and we become the objects of His care.

What about the Trinity?

We have already learned that God is spirit and that He is holy. Therefore, God is the Holy Spirit. We have also learned that Jesus Christ is God (see chap. 5). Therefore, God is Jesus Christ. Yet, while we are correct in identifying Father, Son and Holy Spirit as one and the same God, we would not be correct in saying they are identical and indistinguishable. Jesus distinguished Them. He said, for example, that His followers should **"go and make disciples of all nations, baptizing them in the name of the Father and of the Son and of the Holy Spirit"** (Matt. 28:19).

Jesus *prayed to* His Father as distinct from Himself. **"Not My will but Yours be done"** (Luke 22:42). And He *talked about* the Father as distinct from Himself: **"The Father is greater than I"** (John 14:28).

Similarly, Jesus distinguished the Holy Spirit from Himself and the Father. In fact, He isolated all three in a single statement: **"But the Counselor, *the Holy Spirit*, whom the *Father* will send you in *My* name, will teach you all things and will remind you of everything I have said to you"** (John 14:26).

Jesus was here describing the present age. Jesus Christ was raised from the dead three days after the crucifixion. After 40 days, He ascended into heaven, *where He is now* seated at the Father's right hand (Mark 16:19; Heb. 1:3; 1 Peter 3:22). So both Father and Son are in heaven. But the Father sent the Holy Spirit in Christ's name, and now He is indwelling believers on earth, teaching them and guiding them.

Note, however, that though the Father and the Son are now located in heaven, They are present everywhere. This, of course, is incomprehensible. How can God be one and yet three? How can He be everywhere and yet localized? These questions, and many others, are incapable of resolution by human wisdom. But Jesus clearly teaches these truths and we believe Him.

Jesus said that the Holy Spirit was going to be a great inner source of life to those who believe in Jesus (John 7:38-39). He said the Holy Spirit would convict the world of sin (John 16:8), guide Christians into all truth (John 16:13), glorify Jesus in our midst (John 16:14), empower us to testify to others about Jesus (Acts 1:8), and join us in bearing that witness (John 15:26-27).

Each of these vital ministries of the Holy Spirit merits extended study beyond that which space will here permit. However, the work of the Holy Spirit is discussed to a limited degree elsewhere in this book, for example in the chapter on faith.

What, then, did Jesus say about God?

- To Jesus, God is the Father—loving, forgiving, providing.
- To Jesus, God is the Son, giving Himself for man's redemption.
- To Jesus, God is the Holy Spirit, energizing Christians.
- To Jesus, God is spirit, seeking man's enlightened worship.
- To Jesus, God is absolutely sovereign, almighty.
- To Jesus, God is holy, perfect.
- To Jesus, God is all-knowing.
- To Jesus, God is GOD!

7
What Did Jesus Say About . . .
PRAYER?

In the entrance to our church, I overheard a discussion about music lessons. A master musician could give Debbie some advanced tuba lessons, and even though he charges over $100 per lesson it would be worth it for her to take them. Just three or four lessons from this master could greatly benefit her.

From whom could we learn about prayer better than from the Master Himself? And it won't cost you three figures, either. You already bought the book! I'm not suggesting that the book should have cost you three figures, but Jesus' teaching on prayer is worth that in hard cash, and much more.

The Posture for Prayer

To understand what Jesus said about prayer, we need His elementary as well as His profound teachings. And we need to know both *how* to pray and *why* to pray. So let's begin at the beginning. What's the right posture for prayer? Should we kneel, stand, sit, lie prostrate on the ground, or what?

The Scriptures indicate that various postures are acceptable for prayer. Jesus said, **"And when you *stand* praying, if you hold anything against anyone, forgive him, so that your Father in heaven may forgive you your sins"** (Mark 11:25). That suggests that it's all right to stand and pray.

We read about the Lord Jesus Himself, when He prayed in the garden of Gethsemane, that He withdrew from the disciples about a stone's throw and *kneeled down* and prayed (see Luke 22:41).

70

But in Matthew's account of Jesus' prayer in Gethsemane, we read that Jesus fell with His face to the ground and prayed (see Matt. 26:39). I take that to mean that He was prostrate; He was lying flat on the ground praying. Or maybe He was kneeling as they do in Muslim countries. They kneel, but they're bent over with their faces right against the ground. We're not quite sure of Jesus' posture here, but at least His face was to the ground as he prayed.

The whole discussion reminds me of a poem I read a long time ago. I can't quote it but I always remember the thought. It says people debate whether one should stand to pray, or whether one should sit, or kneel, or fall on one's face, or look up to heaven, but the best prayer I ever prayed was standing on my head—the time I fell in the well!

Certainly it is not the posture of the body but the posture of the heart that counts. And since we have examples in the New Testament of standing, kneeling, and falling on one's face, I conclude that the poet was right. Good praying is not dependent on physical posture.

Jesus had a lot to say, however, about our spiritual posture in prayer. For example, He said that we are to abide in Christ, if our prayers are to be answered. **"If you remain in Me and My words remain in you, ask whatever you wish, and it will be given you"** (John 15:7). He also said we need to be fruitful Christians. **"You did not choose Me, but I chose you to go and bear fruit—fruit that will last. Then the Father will give you whatever you ask in My name"** (John 15:16).

So the posture for prayer is a posture of abiding in Christ, of being in fellowship with Christ, of living so as to bear lasting fruit to His glory.

Jesus also taught that the right posture or attitude for prayer is one of faith and forgiveness. **"Therefore I tell you, whatever you ask in prayer, *believe* that you will receive it, and it will be yours. And when you stand praying, if you hold anything against anyone, *forgive* him"** (Mark 11:24-25).

So this passage tells us two things: What our attitude toward God must be (faith), and what our attitude toward people must be (forgiveness).

In addition to faith and forgiveness, we need humility in prayer. Jesus described a publican and a Pharisee who both went up to the temple to pray. Jesus taught that the only one whose prayer was heard was the one who was humble. **"The Pharisee stood up and prayed about himself: 'God, I thank You that I am not like all other men—robbers, evildoers, adulterers —or even like this tax collector. I fast twice a week and give a tenth of all my income.'**

"But the tax collector stood at a distance. He would not even look up to heaven, but beat his breast and said, 'God, have mercy on me, a sinner.'

"I tell you that this man, rather than the other, went home justified before God. For everyone who exalts himself will be humbled, and he who humbles himself shall be exalted" (Luke 18:11-14).

Notice that the posture of the two men was the same; both stood. But one man approached God with a great sense of unworthiness. He felt he shouldn't even lift up his eyes in the presence of God. He did not argue that he deserved blessing. He did not say, "God, You ought to do this for me, because look at all I've done for You." He came as an unworthy sinner, humbly. And so must we if we are to be heard.

Public and Private Prayer?

Even more than they debate about posture, people like to argue whether prayer should be public or private. That question is one of many concerning which you have to watch out for the "either/or" syndrome. When anyone gives you a choice between "either/or," you always want to ask whether you're being given all your options. Often, you are not. When it comes to deciding between public and private prayer, it's not either/or. It's both.

The Lord teaches very clearly that we're to pray privately. **"When you pray, go into your room, close the door and pray to your Father who is unseen. Then your Father, who sees what is done in secret, will reward you"** (Matt. 6:6).

Whenever I read this, I think of one fellow who threw this statement up to me. I visited his home to invite him to come to church along with his wife who was already attending. "Jesus said we're supposed to pray in the privacy of our own closets," he replied. "I don't need to go to church and parade my religion in front of other people."

I don't know how much of the New Testament he had read,

but apparently he'd gotten as far as the sixth chapter of the first book. If he had read on to chapter 18, he would have discovered that it's not either/or, but it's both. You don't only pray by yourself in your room—certainly, you are supposed to do that—but you also meet to pray with other Christians. **"Again, I tell you that if two of you on earth agree about anything you ask for, it will be done for you by My Father in heaven. For where two or three come together in My name, there am I with them"** (vv. 19-20).

I admit the congregation is small—it says two or three—but I'm sure it includes larger groups also, and it talks about *coming together in Christ's name*. Now, that's a good description or even a definition of the church. The church is where people come together in Christ's name not only to pray but for mutual encouragement in Christ (see Heb. 10:24-25).

Jesus says if you can agree with your brother about your joint petition to God, He will answer. God will answer an individual's prayer, but there's something to be said for corporate prayer, for getting others to share your concerns and for sharing theirs, together bringing these requests to God. Every Christian needs at least one other Christian with whom to pray.

The Basis for Prayer
Any prayer, whether public or private and whatever one's posture, depends on our having a relationship with God through Jesus Christ. We can only come to God, the Bible teaches, through Christ. In three consecutive chapters in the Gospel of John, we are taught that our prayer to God is to be in and through Christ. **"And I will do whatever you ask in my name, so that the Son may bring glory to the Father"** (John 14:13). **"The Father will give you whatever you ask in My name"** (John 15:16). **"I tell you the truth, My Father will give you whatever you ask in My name. Until now you have not asked for anything in My name. Ask and you will receive, and your joy will be complete"** (John 16:23-24; see also v. 26).

So, when we conclude our prayers, "In Jesus' name" or "In the name of Christ," we are praying biblically. Of course, it's possible to repeat those words and have them mean nothing. You are not coming to God in Jesus' name, even if you say the words, if you don't know Jesus. You're a fraud, a counterfeit, if you profess to be coming in Jesus' name but have no authority to use His name because you are not a Christian.

Maybe it's also possible to pray in Christ's name, if you are a Christian, *without* repeating the words. Do I have to end every prayer, or begin it, or some place in it say "In Jesus' name"? Probably not. But I do need to be supremely aware that I am coming to God through Jesus. And it's only natural that I express it in words—at least from time to time.

However, as Jesus made clear, any words we use are meaningless if that's all they are. **"When you pray, use not vain repetitions, as the heathen do. For they think that they shall be heard for their much speaking. Be not ye therefore like unto them, for your Father knoweth what things ye have need of, before ye ask Him"** (Matt. 6:7-8, KJV).

Now, let's be clear on this. Jesus condemned vain repetition and multiplying words in prayer. This seems to call in question ritualistic prayer, certain prayers for certain occasions. It may be possible to use such prayers, if the words we speak are truly coming from our hearts. However, if one speaks the same words frequently, the repetition is likely to be vain—just so many words. And that, Jesus plainly taught we must not do.

A Pattern for Prayer

The Lord's Prayer, as it is commonly known, is recorded both in Matthew 6 and in Luke 11. The form of the prayer varies, it's different in Matthew from Luke. In Matthew, Jesus is recorded as saying, **"This is how you should pray: Our Father in heaven . . . "** (6:9). Luke records that Jesus said, **"When you pray, say: 'Father, hallowed be Your name . . . ' "** (11:2).

The question at this point is, are we supposed to repeat the prayer word for word, or is this a pattern or sample prayer from which we are to learn, an example of the kind of praying we're supposed to do?

From Matthew, one gets the impression that it's the latter—a pattern prayer. **"This is how you should pray."** But from Luke, one gets the impression he is supposed to actually pray these words. **"When you pray, say: 'Father, . . . ' "**

If you come from a ritualistic church, you're probably going to favor the Luke version. If you come from an informal church, you may favor the Matthew version.

I'll just vote for the Bible, and you can take your choice. But one thing is clear: whether we repeat these words or not, we certainly have here a great pattern for prayer.

Jesus gave us this pattern prayer immediately after warning against much speaking, and, notice, the prayer is brief. It's concise. It's to the point. It's also personal and spontaneous. Of course if you memorize it, it's not spontaneous, but the original prayer seems rather spontaneous. It involves talking to God out of the fulness and the needs of one's own heart.

The prayer is also corporate. It says, **"*Our* Father in heaven . . . give *us* today our daily bread."** It is not, "Give *me* my daily bread." It is not, *"My* Father . . . ."* There is certainly nothing wrong with praying, "Lord help me, and solve my problems," but this is a corporate prayer. And it's good, it's right, to be mindful of others as you pray, and to recognize you are part of a body. You are not the only Christian in the world. It isn't just you and God. It's you and your brothers and sisters and God; that's the picture. And this prayer recognizes that.

Notice too that the prayer starts with the focus on God, not on you or your needs. **"Our Father in heaven, hallowed be Your name."** ("May Your name be revered.") Praying ought not to be just running right in to God and saying, "Now, God, I've got this need, and that need, this problem, or that problem; please help me." No, "Hallowed be Your name." Worship. God is supposed to be honored in our prayers.

This is true not only because it's right that God should get first place in our thoughts but also for our own benefit. We profit most from our prayers when we do not focus mostly on us and our needs. We should focus prayer on God and His supply. All that some people do in prayer is recite their problems. They only remind themselves of their woes. They don't remind themselves of God, who is greater than their problems. So prayer does not benefit them as it should.

Note that after worship, the first petition is, **"Your kingdom come, Your will be done on earth as it is in heaven."** A person praying by this pattern takes a while getting around to his own needs. He's preoccupied with God in the first half of his prayer time!

Part of that preoccupation is that God's will might be done "on earth as it is in heaven." Now, most people think prayer is a tool for *getting God to do their will.* That's not what this prayer indicates. It doesn't say, "My will be done in heaven and in earth. Or at least on earth—You can have heaven, but do it my way down here." No, prayer is seeking for God's will to be done.

To some people, "Your will be done" is bad news. That's what they're afraid of anyhow. Who wants to pray *that?* That's what they're trying to *avoid.* But when you get enlightened and find out that God is a God of love and He has a good plan for you, then it's not hard to pray, "Your will be done. I want Your will done in my life, Lord, because that's the best thing that can happen to me. Lord, don't let me foul up Your plan."

Sometimes the thought occurs to people that God's will is going to be done whether they pray or not. This is not so. Specifically, His will may be thwarted in our personal lives if we don't pray. Sinful acts and attitudes, obviously not God's will for His children, may crop up in us precisely because we have not prayed. Jesus said, "Watch and pray so that you will not fall into temptation" (Matt. 26:41).

No doubt, the pattern prayer Jesus gave is tremendous, but it's not super-spiritual. It doesn't talk only about God, as if we have no needs or as if our needs are unworthy of mention. **"Give us today our daily bread."** As famine moves from threat to ever greater reality, this may become more and more a heartfelt prayer. However, even if we live in an affluent society, we need to remember who gives us our daily food. Among other things, this reminds us to be thankful, because God is providing for us. And if sometimes we feel that things are pretty bad, we can still be grateful that at least we're eating.

The prayer next reminds us that we need to treat other people right. We ask God to forgive us for we forgive other people. **"And lead us not into temptation, but deliver us from the evil one."** We're to pray that God will help us to please Him. So prayer is very corrective. People say prayer changes things, and it does. But often the first and most important thing it changes is the person praying, providing he truly prays according to the pattern Jesus gave.

Why Pray?
Jesus' parables on prayer, one in Luke 11 and the other in Luke 18, introduce us to a new dimension of prayer. We've been learn-

ing *how* to pray. Now Jesus is going to tell us *why* to pray.

When Jesus gave His instructions on prayer recorded in Luke 11, He did so on request. He didn't volunteer this information; the disciples asked for it. They said, "Lord, teach us to pray" (v. 1). Notice, they did not say, "Lord teach us *how* to pray." There is a difference. We can know how to pray and never pray. We need not only to know how, but we need to do it. So, Jesus gave His pattern prayer—how to pray—and then He began the process of teaching them to pray. And He did so through two parables.

Shameless Praying

Jesus' prayer parable of Luke 11 has threatened to become my favorite parable on prayer. Perhaps that is because it was a mystery to me until recent times. Now I think I'm beginning to understand it.

"Then He said to them, 'Suppose one of you has a friend, and he goes to him at midnight and says, "Friend, lend me three loaves of bread, because a friend of mine on a journey has come to me, and I have nothing to set before him."

" 'Then the one inside answers, "Don't bother me. The door is already locked, and my children are with me in bed. I can't get up and give you anything." I tell you, though he will not get up and give him the bread because he is his friend, yet because of the man's persistence he will get up and give him as much as he needs.

" 'So I say to you: Ask and it will be given to you; seek and you will find; knock and the door will be opened to you. For everyone who asks receives; he who seeks finds; and to him who knocks, the door will be opened' " (Luke 11:5-10).

Now, get the picture. This fellow has a guest come in the middle of the night to his house. He doesn't have anything to feed him. So he goes next door to his friend's house, knocks, and says, "Give me something to feed my guest." And Jesus makes the crucial point as follows: **"I tell you, though he will not get up and give him the bread because he is his friend, yet because of the man's persistence he will get up and give him as much as he needs"** (v. 8).

The key word in the parable is this word translated *persistence*. In the more familiar King James, it is translated *importunity*. Jesus said that because of his importunity he gets what he wants, not because he's a friend. So we have to understand what the word *importunity* means. Following some of my old bad habits, I always thought I knew what it meant, so I never bothered to research it. Lo, and behold, I looked it up, and it doesn't mean exactly what I thought it meant. I thought importunate prayer simply meant *presistent*. I discovered that it literally means *shameless, impudent, impertinent.**

This fellow has his nerve coming after bedtime to his neighbor asking for something to feed his friend who arrives for a visit in the middle of the night. I mean, surely he had something in the house he could have fed his guest. And if not, this late night visitor wasn't starving to death, was he? He could have waited till morning. The neighbor is in bed, and apparently he's not too prosperous either. It seems he only has one bed, for all his children are in bed with him. And he doesn't really want to help this intruder. But just because the guy has got the sheer brass, the gall to go and ask for it, he gets it. That's what importunity means. And it does take quite a lot of gall to do a thing like this.

What's the lesson for us, then? It seems that Jesus is opening up a whole new area so far as prayer goes. **"Ask and it will be given to you"** (v. 9). You just haven't had the nerve to ask, that's all. You haven't had the gall. You haven't had the brass.

I've been observing how this works even in human experience. I've been embarrassed a time or two because people accompanying me have asked someone to do something for them that I wouldn't have the nerve to ask. I stand there withering, and thinking, *How's this guy going to react?* The surprising thing is that, usually, the guy says OK and does what is requested, just because the other

---

*It seems unfortunate that translators have so often rendered the Greek word *anaideia* simply as *persistent* here. (The word occurs nowhere else in the New Testament, so we cannot compare its use here with other passages.) Grammatically, the term comes from the negation (*an*) of *aideia*, which means *modesty, shame,* or *reverence.* So the word literally means *no modesty, no shame,* or *no reverence.*

Though many popular translations render *anaideia* (mistakenly, I believe) as simply *persistent,* the *Berkeley Version* more properly renders it *brazen insistence* and states in the footnote that it is literally *shamelessness* or *impudence. The New English Bible* makes it *shamelessness,* and *Knox* translates it *shameless asking. Young's Concordance* defines it as *barefacedness.*

fellow had the nerve to ask. Jesus says we're to come to God this way.

That doesn't mean, of course, that we can ask for any outrageous thing that comes to mind. Jesus is hardly teaching us that we all ought to ask for new Cadillacs, or for the usual frivolous things that occur to a shallow mind when we say, "God answers prayer; ask whatever you want." Neither is God going to rescind His own laws by violating another person's will so that the thing we pray for can come to pass . . . as when we pray that a friend will be saved next Sunday at 11:58 A.M.

But there's *something* here for us. The parable clearly implies that we often are not bold enough, or brassy enough, or nervy enough in our praying. And we simply do not have because we do not ask. **"Ask and it will be given to you; seek and you will find; knock and the door will be opened to you"** (v. 9).

This teaching of Jesus can make prayer come vitally alive. Here's a real reason to pray! Many times we go for months and years bereft, deprived of blessings God is perfectly willing to give us, simply because we have not prayed for them. We haven't had enough nerve to pray for them. Or we haven't been concerned enough to pray for them. I've seen this in my own experience, and in the experience of others.

A person might struggle along for a lifetime, impoverished, because he's simply been willing to live on that plain and never had enough nerve to ask God for more. This is not to say that if all who are poor just had enough faith to pray, they'd be rich. But there may be many people who would have much more than they do if they had that much nerve!

A person may go along for years, sick, because he doesn't have enough nerve to ask God to make him well. This is not to make a blanket statement that sickness is the result of lack of prayer, or that you ought to be healed and if you had enough faith you would be. But there may be cases like that.

Here's a person who goes for years in a miserable domestic situation. There is squabbling all the time, or the silence of a cold war. Very possibly neither mate has had enough nerve to ask God to do anything about it.

Another person spends years in a dead-end job, going nowhere. He has just accepted the situation. He hasn't prayed. If he would pray, God might be pleased to answer.

Some people would find their life becoming that—LIFE—if they'd start praying nervy prayers. "Give me a new job. I'm sick and tired of going nowhere." "Give me a new home. This miserable, squabbling, unhappy home I've got—I'm fed up with it." "Give me a new church. I don't want to be part of a church that's just marking time, not going any place."

Prayer of this kind ought not to be superficial or shallow. It involves a spiritual *process*. Suppose I'm trapped in a dead-end job. I've been putting up with it for 10 years. I shouldn't have. I should have prayed this way long ago. But now, I begin to examine my situation.

What does God want for me? That is the first question. (Remember the pattern prayer: "Your will be done.") Does God want me to go through life with my nose to the grindstone hating every day of it? Is that the desire of the good God of love and kindness, who wants to enrich my life, who came to make my life more abundant? (see John 10:10) This whole teaching here in Luke involves what kind of God our God is. Jesus goes on to talk about fathers who know how to be kind to their children. They give them good gifts. Won't your heavenly Father do so much more? (Luke 11:11-13)

So, here I am in this miserable go-nowhere, dead-end job. I say to myself, "What kind of God is God? Would God like to give me something better? Is that God's will?" If I view God as a loving, compassionate Lord who really cares about me, I can only decide it is His will to give me something better.

Now I can begin to pray in faith, shamelessly, "Give me a new job. I expect a new job." Mind you, I'm not just asking for a new job, but I'm asking for it in faith. Why am I asking for it in faith? Because I am convinced God wants to do something for me.

Many people cop out with the phrase, "If it be Thy will," in their prayer. "God, give me a new job, if it be Thy will." But you can't have faith in a situation like that. You don't know if it's God's will or not, so you can't have faith that you are going to get a new job. Decide first whether it's God's will. Then pray shamelessly in faith that God will give you something else, and He will "Ask and you will receive." That is *prayer*.

But notice this: Nobody may know you got a new job, except you. You may be working in the same place, for the same wages, and for the same boss. Probably not, but it's possible. You may have the same old job as far as everybody else is concerned, but you've got a new attitude, a new outlook, and everything's changed.

You pray for a new church, and it might be the same one, but it will be new, different.

You pray for a new home and God will give you a new home. Obviously, it's not God's will that you get your new home through divorce and remarriage. But God can change both you and your mate so that your home is just as new, if not newer, than it would be if you got a different partner. With a different partner, you could very possibly still have the same problems. But God can give you a new home.

"Ask and it will be given to you; seek and you will find; knock and the door will be opened to you. For everyone who asks receives; he who seeks finds; and to him who knocks, the door will be opened" (vv. 9-10).

Persistent Praying

Jesus' other prayer parable teaches what too many translators have tried to make the first parable teach—that we should be persistent in praying. (An altogether too common error is to learn something from Scripture and then to impose that truth on other passages of Scripture whether it fits or not. This effectively blocks additional learning and dwarfs spiritual development.)

"Then Jesus told His disciples a parable to show them that they should always pray and not give up. He said: **'In a certain town there was a judge who neither feared God nor cared about men. And there was a widow in that town who kept coming to him with the plea, "Grant me justice against my adversary."**

" 'For some time he refused. But finally he said to himself, "Even though I don't fear God or care about men, yet because this widow keeps bothering me, I will see that she gets justice, so that she won't eventually wear me out with her coming!" ' " (Luke 18:1-5)

Here is a woman with a problem. She has a need, and she has a legitimate case. She takes it to the judge. He couldn't care less about her. He's a political shyster. We don't know what he's in business for, but it's not to dispense justice. He neither fears God nor worries about men. She has no chance of getting justice from him insofar as his integrity is concerned.

Nevertheless, her pleas are heeded by this judge, for the simple reason that he doesn't want to be continually bothered by her. The judge said, "This woman is going to wear me out. The easiest thing to do to get rid of her is to take care of her demands." And so he did.

What is the point of the story? Jesus gave the point before speaking the parable—men **"should always pray and not give up"** (v. 1). In other words, we ought to persevere. This woman won out, because she refused to give up. If an unjust judge will answer a prayer, solely on the basis of perserverance, will not the kind and just heavenly Father answer your prayers, if you'll persevere?

Clearly, this is instruction, not how to pray, but why to pray. Because if you will persist in a right and just prayer, God will answer it.

Prayer is paradoxical. It is simple enough for the small child to employ, yet deep enough to perplex the most insightful saints of God. We'll be the rest of our lives and perhaps part of eternity understanding what it's all about. The wonderful thing is that we don't have to fully understand it in order to use it. As we learn to pray according to the pattern Jesus gave us, from a proper posture of faith and humility, yet with nerve and persistence, we'll experience a fuller life. Knowing *how* to pray and *why* to pray, we won't be too concerned that we still don't fully know *what* prayer is.

8
What Did Jesus Say About . . .
MONEY?

Many people have trouble with Jesus' parable of the unjust steward (Luke 16:1-8). The problem is that, incredibly, Jesus seems to be commending a rascal.

The story goes that a certain steward or business manager knew he was about to lose his job for mismanagement. Ashamed to beg and not strong enough to dig ditches or work hard for a living, he was on the spot. But he hatched a scheme to provide for himself.

Calling his employer's debtors, he falsified their accounts to their advantage and to the disadvantage of his employer. The idea was that he was buying their favor; he was making them personally indebted to him. Later, when he was out of a job, he would expect help from them in return.

Jesus said, **"The master commended the dishonest manager because he had acted shrewdly"** (v. 8).

Two observations can help dispel the reader's confusion at this point. First, the undiscerning eye, reading the familiar King James text, may think this commendation of the dishonest manager is from the Lord. Not so. It is not from the Lord but from the lord (small *l*). Not from God, but from the man's earthly master. Still, in effect, Jesus does say we should follow the dishonest manager's example: **"I tell you, use worldly wealth to gain friends for yourselves, so that when it is gone, you will be welcomed into eternal dwellings"** (v. 9).

This brings us to the second and more important observation: The master commended the dishonest manager not for his dishonesty but for his shrewd foresight. And it is his foresight, not his dishonesty, that is cited as an example to us.

We have a saying, "Give the devil his due." In this case, the master admired the sagacity of the dishonest manager, however blameworthy his character.

We have trouble with this parable of Jesus because we are too inhibited to use a bad man as an example of something good. Someone might misunderstand us! Jesus took that risk more than once, as, for example, when He made a despised Samaritan the hero of his man-who-fell-among-thieves story (Luke 10:30-37 and see chap. 10).

Jesus' parables imply that we can learn from the worst of men. From this dishonest manager, we learn the most basic principle regarding our relationship to money: *We are to use money to gain imperishable assets for ourselves in the form of eternal friendships.*

Like the manager in the parable we are soon to lose our present positions; we must soon die. Jesus taught that, if we who expect an afterlife are to be as shrewd as many worldly men are, we must see to it that our money has made us friends who will be indebted to us hereafter.

Jesus did set the record straight on the question of honesty as well. After he spoke the parable (vv. 1-8) and isolated the principle (v. 9), He proceeded to emphasize the importance of being honest and trustworthy before God in everything, whether big or small (vv. 10-12). In the process, He as much as says that the whole realm of money is a small thing compared with the powers and privileges to be entrusted to God's people in the life to come. **"So if you have not been trustworthy in handling worldly wealth, who will trust you with true riches?"** (v. 11)

So our handling of money is important. Important enough to warrant a major parable from the lips of Jesus. Important enough to qualify or to disqualify us from greater trusts in the world to come. And the guiding principle is clear: we are to use money to make eternal friends.

Buying friends is not something ordinarily recommended. It usually doesn't work.

The United States tried it for a generation after World War II. Huge sums were spent for foreign aid. Yet, the very countries that received this largess often voted against the United States in the halls of the United Nations.

The same phenomenon can be observed in relations between people, including children (which relations often parallel those between nations!). A child may give his toys away so other children will like him. Or he may buy candy or ice cream for his friends for the same reason. A teenage girl may try to buy a boyfriend's affection by giving him her body. A man may try to win a girl by showering her with gifts. All of these attempts can and often do turn out very badly.

Any gift which is motivated by a desire to *get* is likely to be resented. And well it should be. It is not a gift. It expresses no concern for the recipient but only for the giver's own interests. It is an attempt to exploit others by use of one's money or other means. When anyone gives a gift to get advantage, the gift may be accepted but the giver will probably not be respected, much less loved.

Alexander Solzhenitsyn, the Russian dissident author, said that Americans are regarded with a paradoxical combination of disapproval and admiration by the Russian people. Part of their admiration, he said, was based on the great American generosity demonstrated by aid from America to other nations of the world. But they disapprove of Americans trying to dominate other countries through foreign aid.

Such a mixture of disapproval and admiration on the part of the Russian people would represent a correct analysis of the situation. Common people often have a way of correctly perceiving situations without logically analyzing them. Remarkably, they do this despite the propaganda that inundates them.

What we're saying, it seems, is that you can buy friends with money only if you aren't trying to buy friends with your money!

But how can we use our money to gain *eternal* friendships? Jesus furnished us with specific answers to that question.

Help the Poor

"Sell your possessions and give to the poor. Provide purses for yourselves that will not wear out, a treasure in heaven that will not be exhausted" (Luke 12:33). Giving to the poor will provide Christians with treasure in heaven. How? Very simple. The poor will be standing there to welcome us with outstretched arms of gratitude and friendship. We will have bought their eternal goodwill.

This teaching of Jesus is reinforced by other of His sayings as well. To a young rich man, Jesus said, **"Go, sell your possessions and give to the poor, and you will have treasure in heaven"** (Matt. 19:21).

People have all sorts of excuses for failing to help the poor. "It's their own fault; if they weren't so lazy—if they would get off their backsides and go to work—they wouldn't be poor," or, "I'm not helping those deadbeats; let them get theirs like I got mine."

More subtle, but with the same effect, is the concern often expressed by Christians that a handout is demeaning, that it does more harm than good. Which all sounds reasonable, and perhaps it is. In certain situations, perhaps one should not give to the poor. But to make *not giving* the rule—well, you'll have to argue with Jesus about that! He's the One who said to give to the poor. Maybe He didn't understand people so well as you do?

Many opportunities to help the poor exist. Thanks to organizations such as World Vision, Compassion, and Christian Children's Fund, we can feed, clothe, educate, and evangelize needy orphans in many parts of the world. Who knows whether they will be properly grateful, or whether they will ever express their thanks to us in this life? In eternity, everything will be seen in true perspective. Then, they will know whose money saved them from a bare existence of suffering and privation. Then they are going to feel gratitude and friendship forever toward those who used their money to help them.

Through relief organizations, we can feed starving people in drought and famine ridden areas of earth. World Relief Commission, Sudan Interior Mission, Food for the Hungry, Medical Assistance Programs, and other agencies are actually our servants. They help us to use our money as Jesus said we should—in making eternal friends by giving to the poor.

Medical Assistance Programs also provides us with a way to turn our money into vast amounts of medicines and other health aids for those who could not have them otherwise. If your money becomes a gift of health to some sick and suffering brother, do you think he will forget you in heaven?

Jesus said He will not. Jesus also cautioned, however, that **"when you give to the needy, do not let your left hand know what your right hand is doing, so that your giving may be in secret. Then your Father, who sees what is done in secret,**

will reward you" (Matt. 6:3-4). If giving is intended to impress others or for self-congratulation, it is not giving. It is *buying praise or pride.* As pointed out previously, one can buy friends only if one is not trying to buy friends.

Help the Preacher
Another way to make eternal friends is to use your money to sponsor the preaching of the Gospel. If someone is in heaven because you paid the bills for the preacher, you are going to have an eternal friend.

Jesus said, **"Anyone who receives a prophet because he is a prophet will receive a prophet's reward"** (Matt. 10:41). As the larger context makes clear, *receive* here also means to support materially. Jesus sent His messengers out instructing them, **"Do not take along any gold or silver or copper in your belts; take no bag for the journey, or extra tunic, or sandals or a staff; for the worker is worth his keep"** (Matt. 10:9-10). He proceeded to instruct them how they would be supported in any place they preached: **"Seach for some worthy person there and stay at his house until you leave"** (v. 11).

To receive a prophet, then, meant to provide for him as well. And all who did so were promised a prophet's reward. What is a prophet's reward? No doubt the great joy of meeting friends in heaven who were saved through his ministry. The supporters share in that reward for they shared in making possible that ministry.

What About Worship?
Wheaton, Ill. is a city of churches and Christian organizations, sort of a Protestant Vatican in the eyes of some. One Christian leader commented, "We ought to sell every church building in the city of Wheaton and give the money to the poor." He felt he was reflecting the spirit of Jesus' teaching about money. In this view, money exists to meet people's needs materially and spiritually. It is not right for Christians to build great church edifices while the needs of people go unmet.

Did Jesus say anything about spending money on worship?

Perhaps He did.

A woman once poured on Jesus' head some very expensive perfume. "Some of those present were saying indignantly to one another. 'Why this waste of perfume? It could have been sold for more than a year's wages and the money given to the poor' " (Mark 14:4-5).

Jesus replied, **"She has done a beautiful thing to Me. The poor you will always have with you, and you can help them any time you want. But you will not always have Me"** (vv. 6-7).

Money does not exist *only* to meet people's needs. Far from being wasted, money spent on worship is finding its noblest use. After all, fine things do exist in the world. Are they only to be used in sinful or secular pursuits? What better use could have been made of rare perfume than to employ it in the worship of Jesus? By the same token, why should not the finest materials be used for places of worship, even as they were in Solomon's temple?

Obviously, one can go to extremes in anything. Many churches have developed an "edifice complex." They have so devoted their resources to providing buildings that these have become idols—hindrances rather than helps to worship in spirit and truth.

Nevertheless, it is surely not wrong to spend money for worship.

Avoiding Waste

When Christians wrangle over whether to spend money on worship facilities or evangelism or helping the poor, they miss the mark. God has put plenty of resources in the world to do *all* these worthwhile things. Instead of making the good compete with the good, we ought to urge that the good crowd out the evil. There are certainly enough evil and wasteful uses of money against which to protest!

Jesus gave us the principle. He once fed 5,000 men by miraculously multiplying a boy's lunch of five small barley loaves and two fish. Yet, "when they had all had enough to eat, He said to His disciples, **'Gather the pieces that are left over. Let nothing be wasted'** " (John 6:12).

Why should a Man who could produce unlimited abundance out of a sack lunch concern Himself with conservation or careful management? Only one reason. He was teaching us a principle: let nothing be wasted.

Worse even than waste is the destructive use of money. How many millions of dollars are spent to destroy men's bodies, defile their minds, and damn their souls! There seems to be no shortage of money for the production and purchase of pornography. No shortage of money for films and television programs that tear down morality and undermine the family and home. There is ample money for gambling, including state lotteries. Money is in plentiful supply for abortion mills, narcotics, the tobacco industry, saloons, and nightclubs.

If the money wasted in careless disregard for our resources were added to the money used for destructive purposes and all of it were put to work for God, no one would need to compete for funds for worthy purposes; they would be available in abundance.

Jesus said that right use of money will mean a welcome from many friends in the kingdom of God. In light of that, what will the destructive use of money mean? Jesus said, **"Woe to the world because of the things that cause people to sin! Such things must come, but woe to the man through whom they come!"** (Matt. 18:7) That doesn't sound very encouraging for the person whose money finances the production of "things that cause people to sin." Why, a man should turn to Christ on this issue alone, if there were no other, to escape the woe God has pronounced on those "through whom" evil comes!

Our Own Needs
While the basic principle for use of money is to buy eternal friend-ships, Jesus said there were other legitimate uses for money as well. One such basic and obvious use is to provide for our needs and those of our families. Jesus taught that using funds to care for one's parents in need is an integral part of obeying the command-ment to honor father and mother. The Pharisees had a tradition that could excuse a man from supporting his parents. Jesus condemned such a standard. He said, **"You say that if a man says to his father or mother: 'Whatever help you might otherwise have received from me is Corban' (that is, a gift devoted to God), then you no longer let him do anything for his father or mother. Thus you nullify the Word of God' "** (Mark 7:11-13).

Jesus made allowances for the money demands of living in the world as it is. A man must not only support himself and his family but also pay taxes. Jesus even paid taxes that He had a right to avoid, according to Matthew 17:24-27. He told Peter, **"But so that we may not offend them, go to the lake and throw out your line. Take the first fish you catch; open its mouth and**

you will find a four-drachma coin. Take it and give it to them for My tax and yours." (Since Peter was a fisherman, we might call this an early form of income tax!)

This account, which recognizes the legitimacy and need of our paying taxes, is rich in symbolism. Death and taxes may be inevitable, but they are not the focus of life. In this case, the coin (for taxes) came along with the fish (for sustenance). Taxes and the money to pay them are incidental to life.

Furthermore, even the fish was incidental. Peter's real business was not fishing but following and serving Christ. That's what Jesus taught about money for our personal needs. It's important, but it's really only a side issue. He made that very clear in His Sermon on the Mount. **"Do not worry, saying, 'What shall we eat?' or 'What shall we drink?' or 'What shall we wear?' For the pagans run after all these things, and your heavenly Father knows that you need them. But seek first His kingdom and His righteousness, and all these things will be given to you as well"** (Matt. 6:31-33).

Distortions

Ever since Eden, our adversary the devil has sought to twist and distort men's lives. His influence, in the realm of money, causes us to exactly reverse Jesus' teaching. Instead of getting money to help people, we hurt people to get money. Jesus denounced some religious leaders because **"they devour widows' houses and for a show make lengthy prayers. Such men will be punished most severely"** (Mark 12:40). Whenever we wrong or hurt someone for material gain, whenever we cheat, we reveal that we are 180 degrees removed from the attitude toward money that Jesus said we should display.

But there are other distortions too. We may get our riches honestly but focus upon them as an asset for this life only. To do so is not so much wicked as it is foolish. It is to be outdone by the shrewdness of the dishonest manager of Jesus' parable. It is to be like a rich farmer Jesus described. When his bountiful crops overflowed his barns, he planned to build bigger ones so that he could live in ease and luxury the rest of his life. God addressed this man as "You fool." The man died (was put out of his manager position) and had made no eternal friendships with his abundant means. Jesus said, in applying this tragic story, **"This is how it**

will be with anyone who stores things up for himself but is not rich toward God" (Luke 12:21).

An even greater distortion regarding money is to value it as an end in itself. As foolish as the man is who spends his money only on himself, his folly pales beside that of the man who doesn't spend it at all but hoards it.

Jesus said, **"How hard it is for the rich to enter the kingdom of God! Indeed, it is easier for a camel to go through the eye of a needle than for a rich man to enter the kingdom of God"** (Luke 18:24-25).

Those words were spoken in comment upon a rich young man who had shown, by his unwillingness to give up his money at Jesus' command, that he valued it more than he valued eternal life. His money had not satisfied his spiritual needs for he came to Jesus seeking eternal life. Yet he would not give up his money. The result was inescapable: he went away sad.

The words describing this man are most ironic. "He became very sad, because he was a man of great wealth" (Luke 18:23).

How prevalent is the notion that wealth will bring happiness! Of course, it should! Money gives us great potential. With it, we can spread the Gospel and relieve suffering as well as provide for our own needs. We can have all that money will buy (which is considerable), plus the deep satisfaction of accomplishing worthwhile things.

Jesus said, "It is more blessed to give than to receive" (Acts 20:35). One can't experience this blessing if one has nothing to give. But money, like all of God's gifts to us, can be so distorted by sin that it becomes a curse rather than a blessing. Then we go away sad, not in spite of our wealth, but because of it.

If we are going to avoid finally going away sad because of our wealth, we shall have to pay attention to the words of the Lord Jesus Christ. **"Do not store up for yourselves treasures on earth, where moth and rust destroy, and where thieves break in and steal. But store up for yourselves treasures in heaven, where moth and rust do not destroy, and where thieves do not break in and steal"** (Matt. 6:19-20).

How Much Should We Give?

The Pharisees of Jesus' day were very persnickety about observing the letter of the law. Since the law required them to tithe all their income, they did so down to the gnat's eyebrow. Meanwhile, they were not nearly so careful about their inward moral and spiritual condition.

Jesus said, **"Woe to you, teachers of the law and Pharisees, you hypocrites! You give a tenth of your spices—mint, dill, and cummin. But you have neglected the more important matters of the law—justice, mercy, and faithfulness. You ought to have practiced the latter,** *without neglecting the former"* (Matt. 23:23).

So Jesus taught that there were more important things than their giving an exact tenth of their income, but He also taught that they should have given the tenth of their income.

One of the most compelling accounts concerning giving in all the Scriptures relates to the "widow's mites."

"Jesus sat down opposite the place where the offerings were put and watched the crowd putting their money into the temple treasury. Many rich people threw in large amounts. But a poor widow came and put in two very small copper coins, worth only a fraction of a penny. Calling His disciples to Him, Jesus said, **'I tell you the truth, this poor widow has put more into the treasury than all the others. They all gave out of their wealth; but she, out of her poverty, put in everything—all she had to live on' "** (Mark 12:41-44).

Just as Jesus took notice of what people were giving then, so, we may infer, He takes notice of what we give today.

His comments about their giving certainly have implications for us. Most obviously, He teaches that a small gift from a poor person is a greater sacrifice than a large gift from a wealthy person. Does this not imply that the wealthy ought to give *proportionately* more than the poor, say 15, 25, or 40% rather than a tenth?

Sometimes people become cynical about giving. They perhaps discover or suspect that the funds are not being properly used for the greatest service of God. This can shrivel a person's giving, can become an excuse to withhold funds. It's interesting to observe that the widow was giving her small coins to a corrupt temple system (as even the immediate context reveals; see vv. 38-40). Yet, Jesus commends her.

We have a responsibility to be good stewards, to support the Lord's work through those agencies which we believe best represent Him. But it is far better to give to a less-than-worthy agency than to refuse to give at all. We are giving *to God*. If someone subverts those funds, he will answer to God for it. But we must not let his dishonesty or carelessness dry up our benevolence.

Some have said that Jesus' comments about the widow's gift show He did not support the concept of tithing, that He called instead for sacrificial giving. Perhaps. But for all we know the woman's two coppers *were* her tithe. Being poor, she perhaps had spent 18 coppers to purchase her daily bread and had only this two-copper tithe left.

Her example does perhaps imply that no one is too poor to give. A poor person needs faith to give, for even though the gift is very small, he cannot really afford it. He needs every cent to live on. Thus, it may take a real work of the grace of God to cause a poor person (or anyone) to tithe, but giving is *supposed to be a grace,* not an easy generosity (see 2 Cor. 8:1-7).

But suppose the widow's gift was not her tithe but literally was all the resources she had in this world? What about giving all of one's financial means to the Lord? This is what Jesus required of one would-be follower (Matt. 19:21). Some have tried to apply this as a standard for believers today. Jesus did say, **"Any of you who does not give up everything he has cannot be My disciple"** (Luke 14:33).

When I was growing up in a sawmill town in Central Oregon, I often saw on the streets an old woman we called the Carrot Queen. She was an impoverished widow who kept herself alive by peddling carrots and other vegetables from her small garden. I can still see her in my mind's eye, shabbily dressed, shuffling along the sidewalk, pulling a child's wagon with her produce in it. Along with the carrots, she peddled religion whenever she had the chance.

The story around town was that she would not have had to live as she did. When her husband died, he left adequate provision for her. But "that so-called church got it all." She had given everything away, and now was the town oddity.

I don't know what Jesus thought about the situation. I don't know whether He commended her as He did the biblical widow or condemned the modern day counterparts of the Pharisees who devoured widow's houses (Matt. 23:14), or both. But I do know what her reputation was around town. It was bad. And I know what people thought of the religious group that had taken advantage of her. And that was bad.

It seems apparent that Jesus may sometimes call upon His followers literally to give away everything for His sake. Some have suggested that it would be a great thing if every Christian did this at least once in his life. It would certainly test his faith, cast him upon the Lord, and wean him from the galloping materialism that constantly threatens to choke out the good seed of God's Word in his life.

It seems equally apparent that Jesus does not call everyone to perpetual poverty, which would be the case if one were to give away everything and continue on that plane. Even the small band of disciples had their treasury, undoubtedly with Jesus' approval. And His close friends, Mary, Martha, and Lazarus, maintained a home at Bethany, where Jesus often accepted hospitality. He never hinted, so far as we know, that they should sell out, give away the proceeds, and become paupers.

In fact, there is no record that Jesus ever told anyone to give away everything except the young man alluded to earlier, and he obviously was making an idol of his wealth.

True, Jesus did say we must "give up everything" we have to be His disciples (Luke 14:33). By this, He seems to have meant that we should make no personal claim to our possessions. They must all belong to God. We are to see ourselves as stewards only. And to hold everything we own in an open hand. If God wants us to give it—or to lose it—we are willing, for we have implicitly given up everything.

A cantankerous and selfish rich man, while visiting his pastor was escorted by the preacher to his office window overlooking a busy street. "Whom do you see out there?" asked the preacher.

"I see a lot of men, women, and children," said the rich man.

The pastor then escorted the rich man to a wall mirror.

"Whom do you see now?" he asked.

"I see myself," said the rich man.

"Exactly," said the preacher. "In both cases you looked through a glass, but one sheet of glass had a thin layer of silver behind it. That's all it took for you to be able to see only yourself."

If our silver keeps us from seeing others, we would be better off without it. But if we can see our money as a means of helping others, we will enrich our heaven forever.

9

What Did Jesus Say About . . .

FOLLOWING HIM?

Sometimes people use a special tone of voice and a special vocabulary when they are talking religion. This may suggest that Christianity is not part of everyday living, that it occupies a special compartment distinguished from the real world even by the way one talks about it.

Unfortunately, this attitude can be contagious.

A little boy ran in from the yard to tell his mother he had just seen their dog kill a rat. In his excitement he didn't notice the preacher was visiting. "Mama, Mama," he cried, "Jip got a rat! You shoulda seen him! He grabbed it and shook the stuffin's out of it. Then he let it go, and grabbed it again, and mauled it and shook it till it was—" Just then he noticed the preacher. "Till it was . . . till it . . . till *the Lord took it home!*"

One might almost want to defenestrate a preacher who would have such an effect on a person! Though that would be of the flesh, throwing his jargon out the window might not be a bad idea.

We can't hear the tone of voice in which Jesus called people to follow Him, or prayed, or preached. But we do have a record of the words He used. They were ordinary words, everyday words, not special, churchy words. He simply said, **"Follow Me."**

Occurring some 90 times in the New Testament, the Greek word translated *follow* was used for everything from giving casual directions to a man on the street to calling disciples to a lifetime of dedicated service. In fact, uses of the term almost that widely divergent occur in a single chapter in Matthew.

"And as Jesus passed forth from thence, He saw a man, named Matthew, sitting at the receipt of custom: and He saith unto him, **'Follow Me.'** And he arose and followed Him" (Matt. 9:9, KJV). Matthew *followed* Jesus, as His disciple.

But consider these words a few lines on: "There came a certain ruler, and worshiped Him, saying, 'My daughter is even now dead, but come and lay Thy hand upon her, and she shall live.' And Jesus arose and followed him" (Matt. 9:19 KJV). The Lord Jesus *followed* the ruler, who was simply showing Him the way to his daughter's side.

The same expression in the Greek is used in both situations.

If we want to know what it means to follow Jesus, then, we must look beyond the meaning of the word itself.

Christ Before Family

The opening verses of Matthew 10 record the names of the 12 Apostles whom Jesus "had called unto Him." The subsequent passage outlines His instructions to them. After that, Jesus explained more fully what it would mean to follow Him.

Jesus said, **"Anyone who loves his father or mother more than Me is not worthy of Me; anyone who loves his son or daughter more than Me is not worthy of Me; and anyone who does not take his cross and follow Me is not worthy of Me"** (vv. 37-38).

To follow Jesus requires, then, that we have a supreme love for Him, a love that is greater than our love for those who are naturally dearest to us.

Such a demand by Jesus would be totally out of order were He not God. What presumption it would be for a mere man to thrust himself between parents and children! To alienate the affections ordained from ancient times by God Himself!

The Ten Commandments required God's people to *honor* their parents, but it commanded them to *worship* God (see Ex. 20:3, 12). This same distinction lies behind Jesus' words here. Certainly Jesus would never discourage family love and fidelity. But He demands first place for Himself, the place He must have because He is God, and the place *only* God deserves.

Christ Before Self

Jesus also required His followers to put Him before *themselves*. **"If anyone would come after Me, he must deny himself and take up his cross daily and follow Me"** (Luke 9:23).

Self-denial can be a very superficial thing—like giving up bubble gum during Lent. It can also be a very legalistic, self-righteous thing. "Aren't I godly? I denied myself sleep and prayed all night."

Jesus requires self-denial of His followers, but it is a much more profound and meaningful self-denial than that. Jesus did not say a man must deny himself bubble gum or deny himself sleep or deny himself *anything* in particular. There is no direct object of the verb *deny*. **"If anyone would come after Me, he must deny** *himself.***"**

The natural man affirms himself. Self is the center of his being. Self-centeredness often expresses itself in ugly ways. But it can also express itself in refined ways, as it does when a salesman is very friendly and solicitous of your welfare only so that he may take advantage of you in a sale.

One can perform acts of great kindness or religious devotion, but be motivated entirely by self-interest. To deny yourself sleep in order to afford yourself congratulation is an expression of the self, not a denial of it.

When Jesus said to deny yourself, that is precisely what He meant. There must be a profound shift of your center of being. Previously, you have been at the center of your universe. You have been the sun around which all the planets have revolved. Everything in the universe, even God, if you acknowledged Him at all, was subjugated to your own purposes.

All that must change if you are to be a true follower of Jesus. He is the Sun, the center of the universe, and you with all other planets must revolve around Him.

As undesirable as such self-denial is to the natural man, it is the only way to live in harmony with reality. For the fact is that Jesus Christ *is* the center and focus of all things, and you are not. To place yourself in the center throws everything out of balance.

That is why the self-centered life cannot succeed; balance is as essential to human life as it is to the universe itself and everything in it. Housewives discover the importance of balance when the load gets off center in the washer; it nearly shakes itself to pieces.

Once I was traveling home from Canada to Oregon with a carload of other Bible school students. The engine of our car burned out a rod bearing while we were still some 600 miles from home. Since we had no money to fix it, the mechanic told us he would remove one piston from the engine entirely. It would still run, he told us, on five cylinders instead of six, and *might* get us home.

It ran on five cylinders, but it was out of balance. Over the miles, the car literally vibrated itself to pieces. When the muffler fell off, we began getting sick from the fumes. Still we toughed it out. We were within 50 miles of home when the engine made its last quivering revolution. The car's next stop—the junkyard.

Too many humans have ended on the junk heap because they would not put their lives in balance by placing Jesus at the center instead of themselves. Christ does not want that to happen to any of His followers. He demands we deny ourselves and follow Him.

This basic self-denial Christ-affirmation will lead to specific acts of self-denial. It's even conceivable that God could lead us to give up bubble gum during Lent. If so, such an act of self-denial will be only an expression of the basic ACT of self-denial we made when Jesus Christ became the center of our lives.

Be Dedicated

The follower of Jesus must not only deny himself but he must be unreservedly dedicated to Christ. He cannot be double-minded about it. As the chorus expresses it so well:

> I have decided to follow Jesus;
> No turning back, no turning back.
> Though none go with me, still I will follow;
> No turning back, no turning back."

Not everyone who offers to follow Jesus has this measure of dedication. "As they were walking along the road, a man said to Him, 'I will follow You wherever You go.'

"Jesus replied, **'Foxes have holes and birds of the air have nests, but the Son of man has no place to lay His head'** " (Luke 9:57-58).

I doubt that Jesus spent many homeless nights. Nor were His disciples called to lives of deprivation. These words of Jesus need to be understood in combination with His promises to followers. He told them, for example, **"No one who has left home or wife or brothers or parents or children for the sake of the king-**

dom of God will fail to receive *many times as much in this age* and, in the age to come, eternal life" (Luke 18:29-30).

However, Jesus gave this assurance to those who had already committed themselves to follow Him. It was His response to Peter's statement, "We have left all we had to follow You" (Luke 18:28).

Jesus did not make these "many-times-as-much" promises to would-be recruits. To them, he pointed out the cost involved, not the rewards. Why? Because He wanted followers who were so dedicated to Him that they would follow Him despite the cost, not because of the reward.

Any follower of Christ worth the name considers it his highest privilege to be such. He isn't primarily concerned with what reward he can expect.

The disciple of Jesus is like the kid who would rather play baseball than eat, who then lands a contract to play for more money than he ever imagined earning. Or like the would-be writer who'd almost be willing to pay the publication costs himself just to see his material in print, who then learns that not only will the publisher pay all costs but will pay him royalties for every copy of his book sold.

By contrast, a young man, hearing that there's money in professional baseball, could try to become a baseball player. Or, since there is money in writing, he will be a writer. If the desire is not there for the sake of the activity itself, apart from the rewards, the person is not likely to have the dedication it takes to excel in any field. When he begins to encounter the inevitable difficulties and trials, he will waver if all he wants is the money.

Jesus wants dedicated followers. If news that there will be some hardships along the way discourages a person from following Him, that person is not disciple material.

Jesus tested dedication in other ways besides warning of hardship ahead. He was keenly perceptive of indications of where a prospective disciple's heart was. To one who wanted first to "go and bury my father" and another who wanted to "say good-bye to my family," He spoke severely (Luke 9:59-63). Their interests, their eyes were too much on other things than following the Lord Jesus Christ.

On the other hand, the kind of dedication Jesus requires may be developed in a person who previously had reservations—or even rebelled. One of Jesus' parables illustrates this very well:

"There was a man who had two sons. He went to the first and said, 'Son, go and work today in the vineyard.'

" 'I will not,' he answered, but later he changed his mind and went.

"Then the father went to the other son and said the same thing. He answered, 'I will, sir,' but he did not go.

"Which of the two did what his father wanted?" (Matt. 21:28-31)

Obviously, the son who repented of his disobedience and went to work in his father's vineyard better represents a dedicated Christian than the son who talked obedience but did nothing.

Lloyd Cory, while a young man, once played his trumpet where Paul Fleming, founder of New Tribes Mission, heard him. Fleming told young Cory, "God needs that instrument down in South America."

"OK," said Lloyd, "I'll send it down!"

Not only was Lloyd unwilling to go work in the Lord's vineyard, but he was flippant about it. But his experience in the military during World War II led Lloyd to dedicate his life to Christ. Though he never went to South America, he does guide the entire editorial department of Scripture Press, whose ministry extends around the world.

Be Disciplined

Dedication is one thing; discipline is another. Distraction is the great enemy of both. Their easy distraction by other things revealed the lack of dedication of some would-be disciples. With the Twelve, it was different. Their dedication was beyond question. Yet because they sometimes lacked disciplined minds, they were distracted to the point of endangering their effectiveness as followers of Jesus.

One of the chief distractions to which the disciples were subject was the actions and attitudes of others. Peter fell into this, even when he was on his best behavior as a result of his humiliating failure in denying the Lord three times. The Lord had restored Peter to fellowship and commissioned him to once again **"Follow Me!"**

"Peter turned and saw that the disciple whom Jesus loved was following them. . . . When Peter saw him, he asked, 'Lord, *what about him?*' Jesus answered, **'If I want him to remain alive until**

I return, what is that to you? You must follow Me' " (John 21:20-22).

"What about him?" is a question asked far too often by Christians.

It may be asked in idle curiosity. We simply like to be in the know. This desire is a basic trait of human nature, exploited immensely by Hollywood gossip columnists, for example, who offer readers the latest private tidbits of information about the stars.

Nearly every office or plant has its busybody type whose chief occupation is to keep tab on everyone else. Every neighborhood seems to have its prying eyes. All this is of "the flesh" and has no place in the life of the Christian. Jesus says, **"What is that to you? You must follow Me."** The sad fact is that the undisciplined mind, occupied with idle curiosity about others, will not be effectively fulfilling its task in the service of Christ.

"What about him" may sometimes be asked more in self-defense than curiosity. One may point to others in order to rationalize one's own failures or sins. It should be obvious, at least to every parent, that this is a mark of immaturity. Our children will very often make it their defense for wrongdoing.

"Suzie, did you hide your little brother's baseball? Shame on you!"

"What about him? He threw my doll on the floor!"

How childish we must appear to God when we justify our wrongdoing on the basis of what others have done. We claim to be following Him who said, **"If you do good to those who are good to you, what credit is that to you? . . . But love your enemies, do good to them, and lend to them without expecting to get anything back"** (Luke 6:32, 35).

This, of course, is much easier said than done. Another person's wrong may seem to justify our retaliation. Is he to be allowed to just get away with it?

Depending on the circumstances (particularly whether we are in some position of authority or responsibility in the matter), it may be that we should act against the wrongdoing of another. If someone was robbing your house, wouldn't you call the police? If you *were* a policeman, wouldn't you arrest a robber in your own home?

Those actions against evil would be right. The problem is that when others do wrong, we may thus be distracted from the Lord.

Our attention becomes so focused on them (instead of Him) that all we can think of is to punish them. Even if the punishment is justified, we become wrong in our relationship with the Lord. We are no longer following Him; we are pursuing them.

This error can overtake the most sincere Christians. A respected minister once wrote a tract that lovingly persuaded readers to become Christians. He entitled it "Come to Jesus."

Sometime later he became engaged in a dispute with another Christian leader who verbally abused him. At length, the minister prepared for publication a scathing attack on his adversary. He asked a close friend to read the proofs. The friend was dismayed by the unloving, harsh spirit exhibited in the writing but hardly knew how to rebuke his brother without seeming to betray him.

"Well, how did you like it?" asked the writer. "It really demolishes my opponent, don't you think?"

"It certainly is powerful writing," agreed his friend. "You know, I couldn't help contrasting it with your tract. If you publish this, I think an appropriate title would be: 'Go to the Devil,' by the author of 'Come to Jesus.' "

It was a blow well struck. The minister saw his own unChristlike spirit, and an ugly episode was avoided.

"What about him" can also express an improper trust in or dependence upon others. The psalmist said, "It is better to trust in the Lord than to put confidence in man. It is better to trust in the Lord than to put confidence in princes" (Ps. 118:8-9).

New Christians often make this mistake, as do older Christians who have never matured. They exalt their leaders or other "spiritual" Christians too much. They decide right and wrong for themselves on the basis of what these admired Christians do.

So and so is such a good Christian, and he does it, so surely it must be all right.

But Jesus did not say to follow so and so. He said, **"Follow Me."** What Jesus permits another to do, He may forbid to you. Or vice versa. He has that right, you know.

Furthermore, every Christian has failings. And the more you idolize other Christians, the more likely you are to be hurt when you discover their failings. Probably you will then make your second major mistake and decide that they are hypocrites. You may suspect all Christians are hypocrites, and you may turn away even from Jesus.

The fact is you had already turned away from Jesus to a degree without realizing it. You had been distracted from Jesus by your admiration for or dependence on another Christian. Now you are distracted from Jesus by your disappointment with another Christian. What griefs and errors you would save yourself if you would listen more attentively to Jesus' words, **"Follow Me."**

Of course, you intended to follow Jesus. What happened? You didn't maintain a disciplined mind. You allowed yourself to be distracted.

Following Jesus is like driving on the freeway. You have to pay attention to what you are doing. The freeway is well marked. Signs notify the motorist of approaching exits at intervals up to several miles ahead. But if one is distracted by others in the car, it's easy to zoom right on by. The first thing you know, you are in the wrong place, going farther from your destination every moment, and having no simple way to get back on course.

If we are to be true followers of Jesus, what will it mean for us in terms of our daily lifestyle?

Remember playing "Follow the Leader" as a child? You were required to do precisely what the leader did. If he hopped on one foot, you hopped on one foot. If he crawled under the fence, you crawled under the fence. If he put one hand behind his back and the other on top of his head and whistled as he walked, you did the same. And if it was his right hand behind his back and his left hand on his head, you must not reverse the order.

Quite simply, then, to be a follower of Jesus, is to *follow* Him, doing precisely as He would do. "As He is, so are we in this world" (1 John 4:17, KJV). The problem with Christianity today is there are too many "followers" who aren't following, too many "believers" who won't believe God, and too many "Christians" who are nothing like Christ.

Jesus said, **"Whoever serves Me must follow Me; and where I am, My servant also will be"** (John 12:26).

Some people imagine they can serve Christ without following Him. Some who are not even Christians would like to think they occasionally render Christ a service. They may contribute money to the church or work on the church property or help a Christian who is in need.

As good as these actions seem, Jesus says we are no servants of His unless we follow Him. And that requires us to be with Him.

The Rewards

Often a person who talks too much repulses others. Sometimes, though, such a person comes in handy. He blurts out the question we wanted to ask but didn't dare. He risks the embarrassment, but we get our answer.

The Apostle Peter is well known for speaking first and thinking later. He asked the question many other Christians sooner or later might like to ask: *If I follow Christ, what's in it for me?* Or, as Peter put it, "We have left everything to follow You! What then will there be for us?" (Matt. 19:27)

It was a fair, if indelicate, question, and Jesus answered it. He told the apostles they would sit on 12 thrones judging the 12 tribes of Israel. He then proceeded to answer the same question as it applies to us. **"And everyone who has left houses or brothers or sisters or father or mother or children or fields for My sake will receive a hundred times as much and will inherit eternal life"** (Matt. 19:29).

Jesus followed that promise with one of the enigmatic statements He liked to use on various occasions. **"But many who are first will be last, and many who are last will be first"** (v. 30).

This veiled statement becomes powerfully clear when one considers it in connection with the parable which follows. Unfortunately, the parable is placed in a separate chapter by those who long ago arranged the biblical text into chapters and verses. (The original text did not have these divisions, and, while they are very helpful in locating passages and are usually placed appropriately, they sometimes hinder understanding by placing a break where none should exist.)

In this case, the division between the 19th and 20th chapters of Matthew is particularly unfortunate. The statement concluding chapter 19 can hardly be understood without the parable, and the parable can hardly be understood without the background of Peter's question and our Lord's reply.

The parable concerns workers in a vineyard. Though they are hired at various hours through the day, when it comes time to pay them in the evening, all receive equal wages. As though this were not bad enough, those who worked the full day had to stand in line and receive their money last. Those who started work at 5 P.M. and quit at 6 P.M. not only got a full day's pay, but they got it first.

Jesus tied this parable to the 19th chapter (even though others have separated them) by repeating at the end of the parable the same saying which preceded it: **"So the last will be first and the first will be last"** (20:16; 19:30).

The key to understanding the parable lies in the question of Peter (19:27), "What then will there be for us?" and in the key words of 20:2, 13, *agreed, agree.*

The whole passage is a warning against the intrusion of a mercenary spirit into the life of a follower of Jesus.

You see, there was a time when Peter would never have asked his question, "What then will there be for us?" He didn't begin following Jesus with an eye to what he might gain by it. He considered it the greatest of privileges to follow Jesus. He'd have gladly paid Jesus to let him be a disciple.

When Peter was new in his relationship to Christ, he properly counted himself unworthy to be a follower of the Master. After Jesus showed His divine power by giving Peter and his companions a miraculous catch of fish, Peter "fell at Jesus' knees and said, 'Go away from Me, Lord; I am a sinful man!' " (Luke 5:8)

It is a different spirit that threatens to engulf Peter now as he wants to know what his benefits are going to be. Before, if he thought of reward at all, he was quite willing to leave the whole question to the love, fairness, and generosity of the Lord. Now he almost seems to want a union contract, an agreement with the Lord about what he is to receive.

Jesus' parable, then, deals with a master who makes an agreement with his workers—to give a day's pay for a day's work (20:2). Note, however, that there was no such agreement made with those who were hired later in the day. To them, the master proposed an arrangement such as Peter previously had. **" 'You also go and work in my vineyard, and I will pay you whatever is right' "** (v. 4).

Note too that those hired the eleventh hour were not deadbeats but had simply not been fortunate enough to find a job (vv. 6-7).

At the end of the day, the master kept his agreement with those who had an agreement. However, those who simply worked without a contract, trusting the master and considering the work a privilege, received much more in proportion to their labors, and they received it first.

The lesson is plain. Nobody will ever lose out by serving Christ.

But those who serve Him gladly, with no calculating eye on their benefits, will discover Him at last to be a generous Lord who delights to bestow rewards abundantly.

Here Too

The rewards of the follower of Christ do not all await the end of the day's labor. Jesus said, **"I am the light of the world. Whoever follows Me will never walk in darkness, but will have the light of life"** (John 8:12).

For the Christian, life makes sense. It all hangs together. He has a purpose for being. Everything that happens to him fits a divine pattern. He can't always see the pattern, but he can see the Pattern-maker. Light invades all his darkness, because he knows all things work together for good for him.

Those who do not follow Christ have glimpses and flashes of light in their darkness, perhaps, but they really don't know what life is all about.

Two men stand in this world's twilight. One becomes a follower of Jesus. He begins to walk in light even now, and he is en route to eternal day. The other goes his own way. He stumbles into deeper and deeper shadows even now, and he is en route to eternal night.

Best of All

A little phrase tucked away in one of Jesus' sayings epitomizes how wonderful it will be hereafter to have followed Jesus here. **"Whoever serves Me must follow Me; and where I am, My servant also will be. *My Father will honor the one who serves Me"*** (John 12:26).

What will it mean to be thus honored by the Father?

A man graduates from college with honors, and it means something. From that day on, whenever he submits a resumé for a position or a biographical sketch for publicity purposes, he is the man who graduated with honors—*cum laude,* or *magna cum laude.*

A man serves his country with rare distinction, and is honored with a medal. If he is an American and merits the country's highest award, he gets the Congressional Medal of Honor. That means something! It's not conferred on every citizen who pays his income taxes. If you had a Congressional Medal of Honor, it would surely be mentioned in your listing in *Who's Who.*

Mothers of the year, citizens of the year, citations, awards, honor rolls, Phi Beta Kappa keys, National Honor Society memberships, valedictorians, salutatorians, doctorates, titles, degrees—all testify to the value humanity places on receiving honors.

What would it mean then to be honored not by earth's prestigious institutions but by the Supreme One Himself?

Jesus said, **"My Father will honor the one who serves Me."**

An episode from the Old Testament Book of Esther brings vivid dimension to this prospect of being honored by God the Father. Haman, the implacable foe of the Jews, had plotted the death of God's entire people, wherever they might be scattered throughout the empire of Ahasuerus. He was particularly incensed, however, against Mordecai, who had refused to kneel to him. For Mordecai, Haman built a gallows 80 feet high, on which he was determined to see Mordecai hanged.

It just so happened that the very night before Haman was to ask King Ahasuerus for the death sentence on Mordecai the king could not sleep. It was one of those coincidences in which one can so clearly see the hand of God (though the name of God is nowhere mentioned in the Book of Esther).

Since he couldn't sleep, Ahasuerus decided to read the chronicles of his kingdom. Maybe he figured that if anything could put him to sleep it ought to be the history book! He "just happened" to read the account of an incident in which Mordecai had rendered a great service to the crown. Mordecai had caught wind of a plot against the king. He had reported it, the traitors were apprehended, and the kingdom was saved. But Mordecai had never been honored for his service.

The next morning, while Ahasuerus was still wondering what he could do to honor Mordecai properly, Haman made his appearance, intending to ask for Mordecai's execution. He never got around to it.

Ahasuerus asked Haman, "What shall be done unto the man whom the king delighteth to honor?"

Haman thought, "To whom would the king delight to do honor more than to myself?"

Since he thought it was for himself, Haman suggested the best and highest honors he could think of. Let the man to be honored wear the king's own apparel; let him ride the king's horse through the main street of the capital city, wearing the king's crown on his head. Let one of the king's noblest princes walk before the honored hero, proclaiming to everyone, "Thus shall it be done to the man whom the king delighteth to honor."

Guess which of the king's noblest princes got the assignment to escort Mordecai through the streets with praise!

The words must have been devastating as they fell on Haman's ears. "Make haste, and take the apparel and the horse, as thou hast said, and do even so to Mordecai the Jew" (6:10).

All of this provides a wonderful parable for today's Christian. The world may little favor a follower of Jesus. It may indeed hate him and consider him only good enough for hanging. It may prepare its gallows and rear them high, planning for the Christian's destruction. But the King will order otherwise. With the noblest tributes the mind of man can imagine the King will sooner or later honor those who truly follow Jesus.

Jesus said, **"My Father will honor the one who serves Me."**

10
What Did Jesus Say About . . .
RELATING
to OTHERS?

People are funny.

Let a national disaster occur—an earthquake, a killer storm, a volcanic eruption—and nations all over the world rush relief supplies to the victims. But the very nations which send disaster relief may turn around and inflict disaster on other nations through war.

Let a personal calamity occur—a family's house burns, a child falls into a well—and neighbors hurry to the rescue. Yet the same neighbors may feud against each other to the point of literally destroying one another.

People can be very kind, compassionate, and loving, but they can also be vicious, hateful, even murderous. And often it's the *same people* manifesting these opposite characteristics. How inconsistent we are!

Jesus told us what to do about both of these tendencies. We should nurture the potential for compassion in ourselves and others, and we should check the potential for hate and hurt.

Jesus said that the second greatest of all commandments is that we should love our neighbors (Matt. 22:38). That is the basic rule: *our relationships with others are to be based on love.* And if we want to know who "others" includes, we can begin by considering Jesus' parable of the Good Samaritan (Luke 10:25-37).

Loving some people can be extremely difficult—seemingly out of the question, in fact. "Love my neighbor? Of course, but just who all does that include?"

Such was the question of the lawyer whose inquiries gave rise to Jesus' parable.

Jesus' reply was a scorcher. He told a story which reversed the roles that were traditional to their minds. Instead of making a respected priest or Levite a hero, He made them the villains. And the hero was a despised Samaritan. The impact of that casting is difficult for us to appreciate, not being immersed in their culture. It is almost as if a preacher were to tell a story in which a Baptist and a Nazarene were villains and an atheist was the hero.

The story itself is simple enough. A traveler is robbed and beaten. Respected religious leaders of the Jews simply pass by this stranger in need, but a member of a half-breed, doctrinally corrupt tribe stops to render assistance, at considerable inconvenience to himself. The story implies that the "neighbor" whom we are to love includes *anyone we happen to encounter,* even a foreigner or a stranger.

Undoubtedly we need to show more love to strangers. The Bible says that "by so doing some people have entertained angels without knowing it" (Heb. 13:2). Hospitality, especially friendliness toward strangers, is one grace in which residents of Eastern countries generally outshine those in the West. And the hospitality of ancient times seems to have far exceeded that which is customary now. Industrialized society apparently leads to an impersonal society. If the influence of Christianity were as strong on western culture as the influence of industrialization, we could counteract this trend.

The problem is that we tend not to see strangers as people. An extreme form of this depersonalization may be observed in the people who go on killing sprees across the country. Such killers seem to be heartless monsters, but they are not necessarily so. They may be capable of compassion and kindness. Some may in fact be soft-hearted persons who weep over the death of a pet dog or buy an expensive gift for a child acquaintance. Their problem is that they do not see their victims as real people.

We tend to do the same thing when we engage in war. The enemy is depersonalized. Thus gentle boys from back home become brutal killers, sometimes massacring men, women, and children, whom they see not as flesh and blood human beings like their own parents, wives, and kid sisters but as the *enemy,* an impersonal opposing force.

Our insensitivity to one another is a milder manifestation of the same depersonalization that affects the killers. We don't care about strangers. Jesus says we are to care for others, whoever they are, even if they are very unlike us and even if they are unknown to us.

One of the friendliest, most personable men I know is Dr. John E. Haggai of Evangelism International. Dr. Haggai is sometimes misunderstood in the United States because in his zeal for the international work God has given him he can appear to be rather egotistical. And his friendliness to rich and important people can seem to be self-seeking.

Yet, as I learned in traveling around the world with him, John is as kind and friendly to insignificant strangers as he is to important officials. When we rode in a hotel elevator, he would speak to the lowly operator as graciously as I had seen him speak to countless dignitaries.

I commented on this somewhat skeptically. Haggai admits to owning over 40 books on salesmanship, and figuring he had read them studiously, I said, "If a person wants to win friends and influence people, he has to take an interest in them."

"Yes," he replied at once, "but if one works on that principle, he is kind only to those people he wants to win or influence. The thing is to be kind to everyone, whether he can do anything for us or not, and even if we never expect to see him again."

Friends and Enemies

We tend to leave strangers out of our personal worlds altogether, and this violates the law of love. Those individuals whom we do admit, willingly or grudgingly, to our worlds, become either friends or enemies. We automatically divide people into these two groups: those who are with us and those who are against us. Jesus says we are to *love both*.

"You have heard that it was said, 'Love your neighbor and hate your enemy.' But I tell you, love your enemies and pray for those who persecute you, that you may be sons of your Father in heaven. He causes the sun to rise on the evil and the good, and sends rain on the righteous and the unrighteous. If you love those who love you, what reward will you get? Are not even the tax collectors doing that? And if you greet only your brothers, what are you doing more than

others? Do not even pagans do that? Be perfect, therefore, even as your heavenly Father is perfect" (Matt. 5:43-48; see also Luke 6:32-36).

As we tend to depersonalize strangers, we tend to dehumanize enemies. Strangers are not real people to us. Our enemies by contrast are real enough, but they are despicable. So, to some of the "beautiful people" of the counterculture, policemen were not humans; they were pigs.

Patricia Hearst spoke in beautiful terms about her loving companions in the Symbionese Liberation Army. She also spoke lovingly about the people, the masses of Americans being ripped off by the oppressive power structure. But her own parents, now her enemies, were "the pig Hearsts." In taking this attitude, Patty was not so different from everyone else in the world. Love your own and hate your enemy is the world's standard.

Jesus said it was not to be the standard for the Christian. And He cited God Himself as the Christians' example: God **"is kind to the ungrateful and wicked. Be merciful, just as your Father is merciful"** (Luke 6:35-36).

As one might expect, Jesus had difficulty in getting His disciples to understand such a revolutionary attitude toward one's enemies. Actually to *love* them?! Earlier we mentioned the low esteem in which Jews held Samaritans. Naturally, the feeling was mutual. Samaritan prejudice against the Jews was so great that Samaritans would not accommodate travelers who were en route to Jerusalem.

When a certain Samaritan village declined to welcome Jesus because He was on His way to Jerusalem, the disciples were ready to retaliate. James and John asked, "Lord, do You want us to call fire down from heaven to destroy them?" (Luke 9:54)

But Jesus turned and rebuked them. **"Ye know not what manner of spirit ye are of. For the Son of man is not come to destroy men's lives but to save them"** (vv. 55-56, KJV). The people Jesus came to save included even His enemies.

This concept of loving one's enemies is revolutionary to say the least. The Judaism of Christ's day said "Love your neighbor and hate your enemy" (Matt. 5:43). Other great religions of the world have been just as far from Christ's "love your enemies" as that Judaism was.

K. M. Usman of India was once a Muslim priest. He began to

compare Jesus Christ as revealed in the New Testament with Muhammad as he is revealed in the Koran. Muhammad was persecuted by an uncle who threw stones at him and an aunt who put thorns where he would be walking barefoot. She also threw garbage on him when he was going to morning prayers. Muhammad prayed, "Cursed be the two hands of Abu Lahab, and he will perish. His wealth and what he has earned shall avail him not. Soon shall he enter into the blazing fire, and his wife too, who goes about slandering. Around her neck shall be a halter of twisted palm fiber."

With that prayer of Muhammad, recorded in the Koran, Usman compared the prayer of Jesus when He was suffering the infinitely greater atrocity of the cross. Instead of praying curses on His enemies, Jesus said, **"Father, forgive them, for they do not know what they are doing"** (Luke 23:34).

Usman concluded that Muhammad's reaction was that of an ordinary human being and that Jesus' reaction in the midst of such extreme suffering was only possible if He were divine. Usman is now a Christian evangelist, working near Agra, site of the world famous Taj Mahal.

Yes, Jesus taught us to love our enemies, and His teaching was not empty theory or mere high sounding words that have never worked and are unworkable. Jesus loved His enemies, thus supplying us an example that we should love not only as God the Father does but as Jesus Christ the man does.

Yet, the admonition to love our enemies as God does is not without difficulties, for *God will at last consign His enemies to eternal punishment*. If we are to emulate God's kindness toward His enemies, are we also to emulate His wrath?

There is at least a hint in the teachings of Jesus that we *are* to contemplate a time when our love for the enemies of God will properly be replaced with judgment. Jesus said to His disciples once, **"If anyone will not welcome you or listen to your words, shake the dust off your feet when you leave that home or town. I tell you the truth, it will be more bearable for Sodom and Gomorrah on the day of judgment than for that town"** (Matt. 10:14-15).

How are we to reconcile this with "love your enemies"? If we loved people would we call down on them a judgment more severe than that which obliterated the accursed cities of Sodom and Gomorrah? Yet, that is what Jesus instructed His disciples to do.

We could seek an answer by saying that these who rejected the disciples' message were not their personal enemies. Instead they were choosing, by their rejection of the Gospel, to be enemies of Christ. The implication of such an argument is that it is not right to hate one's own enemies but it is right to hate God's enemies. That hardly seems a satisfactory answer.

In the first place, we are all enemies of God until His grace saves us (see Rom. 5:6-10; 8:7). In the second place, the situation with the Samaritan village, cited earlier, is almost exactly parallel to this one. It was not for personal enmity against the Samaritans that James and John wanted to call down fire, but because they were rejecting Christ. Yet Jesus rebuked their vindictiveness.

Let's sort out the facts.

1. We are commanded to love our enemies.

2. Jesus loved and prayed for His enemies.

3. Jesus told His disciples to testify against those who rejected Christ, and that this would result in their severe judgment hereafter.

4. God's wrath will abide forever on those who finally reject Christ.

It seems that one rule applies to now, another to hereafter. God acts in love toward everyone now, and so should we. But God will punish the wicked hereafter, and we will concur.

This life is a probationary period. People can change—and often do. Jesus came to save men's lives. Love can often win men's hearts and change them. Man's destruction could hardly be expected to accomplish the same ends. And we can never tell who will repent and be saved and who will perpetuate his enmity against God and be forever lost. Therefore, it is our business now to reflect God's grace and love. We are to be motivated only by good will toward everyone. We are to be concerned for the welfare of everyone.

Misusing One Another

Jesus also made it clear that Christians are supposed to manifest a special love for other Christians. **"A new commandment I give you: Love one another. As I have loved you, so you must love**

**one another. All men will know that you are my disciples if
you love one another"** (John 13:34-35).

Our love for one another often doesn't stand a chance. Other
dynamics are operating so strongly that love is crowded from the
scene. For example, we are often too busy *resenting* people to
love them.

Jesus provided for the resolution of problems between Christians, problems that left unresolved spawn resentment and crowd
out love. He said, **"If your brother sins against you, go and
show him his fault, just between the two of you. If he listens
to you, you have won your brother over"** (Matt. 18:15).

This passage is cited frequently but followed rarely. It provides
remedies that almost make the cure seem worse than the disease.
That is, if your brother fails to heed your appeal, you are to confront him next in the presence of witnesses. If he still refuses to
repent, you are to hail him before the church. And if he then
remains adamant, he is to be disfellowshiped (see Matt. 18:16-
17).

The procedure makes sense for dealing with serious problems
in a fellowship of Christians, and no doubt it ought to be followed
more than it is. But most problems between people are comparatively trivial. It seems absurd to make a church case out of
them.

For example, someone speaks a word of rebuke to your child
for acting up in the church building. You don't appreciate it because rebuking your child is your prerogative and furthermore
you don't think his behavior was that serious. Should you make an
issue of this—perhaps even split the church—trying to decide who
is right or wrong? Who really needs to be rebuked and repent?
Some could feel you do for allowing your child to misbehave.

I doubt you should always confront a person you feel has
wronged you. But neither should you allow resentment to grow
in your heart until you cannot love him.

Rather than viewing these instructions of Jesus about confronting a brother as a rigid rule applying to every interpersonal problem (which rule we usually ignore), perhaps we ought to ask
the intent of His words. (See chap. 3 for a discussion on the
relative importance of the letter of the law on the one hand and
the spirit or intent of the law on the other.)

The context of this rule has to do with the unity and fellowship that should exist between Christians. Being able to pray together and to worship together is a precious privilege (see Matt. 18:19-20). We have already read that love between Christians is to be apparent to the world, a testimony of the reality of Christ in us (John 13:34-35). When one Christian sins against another, all of these values are jeopardized. Resentment and love cannot coexist. Sin needs to be dealt with so that resentment might be dissolved and Christian unity preserved.

But confronting one who has wronged me and securing his repentance is *not the only way* of overcoming resentment. Perhaps I can simply overlook the offense. Perhaps I can give my brother the benefit of the doubt, attribute a benevolent motive to him, and forget the whole thing.

One reason to confront a brother who sins against me is to resolve my resentment. Another reason may be to help him overcome his fault (**"go and show him his fault"**). To return to the example of the rebuked child, suppose the adult is a meddling, grouchy person who is turning children against church and driving whole families away by his unkind and high-handed behavior. Perhaps he needs to be confronted about it, for his own sake and for the sake of the whole church.

On the other hand, if the action was untypical, or perhaps more to be praised than blamed in the opinion of half the congregation, why cause trouble? It's hard enough to "show him his fault" if a person is clearly in the wrong, human nature being what it is. You'll have little chance showing him his fault if it's not clear that that's what it is!

The important principle to remember here is: *Never harbor resentment.* If you can simply forgive and forbear, accepting others with their weaknesses even as you want to be accepted with yours, good. If the thing bothers you too much to just forget it, pray about it. Maybe God will dissolve it, especially when you consider how much He has forgiven you and how inconceivable it is that you should refuse to forgive anyone else (see Matt. 18:21-35).

But if your resentment cannot be dissolved any other way, confront your brother. Hard as that is, and risky as it is, it's better than harboring resentment. Better to take action that risks an open break in fellowship than to follow a course of nonaction that guarantees broken fellowship by perpetuating a resentment that already exists.

Judging People

"I know we shouldn't judge, but . . . ." That is how too many gossip sessions begin. If we shouldn't judge, let's not judge.

Sometimes the person who says, "I know we shouldn't judge, but . . ." is not so mistaken in what he says afterwards as in what he understands by that statement. Jesus said, **"Do not judge, or you too will be judged"** (Matt. 7:1-2). People often interpret that statement of Jesus to mean one should never voice critical opinions about others . . . or even form such opinions.

Whatever Jesus meant when He said not to judge, it could not be that we are to have no opinion whatever of other people. In that sense, we inescapably "judge" everyone we encounter. Obviously, I must form *some* impression when I meet another. I have a generally favorable or generally unfavorable impression of every person I meet.

If I have good sense, however, to say nothing of Christian charity, I mistrust my impressions. I know that people are not always what they seem. Faults I detect may be inconsequential, while strengths I don't detect may be basic. So I must not permit myself to judge people.

This does not mean I refuse to judge people's actions, however. If I catch a person in a lie or hear him tell an obscene story or use God's name in vain, there is no reason for me to pretend those actions are anything but sins.

For me to condemn an action condemned by God's Word is not a judgmental act on my part. It is simply a case of accepting God's judgment which He has already clearly expressed. Indeed, I am not only justified in condemning such action but I am expected to do so. Scripture speaks against some because, "although they know God's righteous decree that those who do such things deserve death, they not only continue to do these very things, but also approve of those who practice them" (Rom. 1:32).

Jesus commended the church in Ephesus for condemning sin. **"But you have this in your favor: You hate the practices of the Nicolaitans, which I also hate"** (Rev. 2:6). Note that He commended them for hating certain *practices,* not hating the people involved in them.

It is appropriate, then, to disapprove certain actions of others. We need to be sure, however, that the action in question is something clearly condemned by God's Word and not simply something contrary to our tradition. Jesus was constantly being judged by His enemies for violating their rules, which, though merely traditions of men, assumed all the force of moral law in their minds.

Examples of misjudging the actions of others abound today. A member of a traditional church was very upset when he discovered that the informal church to which his fiancee belonged had scheduled no Christmas Eve service. He had never heard of such a thing and thought it a terrible desecration of the holiday. Little did he realize that Christmas itself is traditional, the date of Christ's birth being unknown. Indeed some, including Puritans in the American colonies, have considered any Christmas observance to be pagan.

I once received a blistering attack from an anonymous letter writer for conducting a nontraditional wedding ceremony. She had heard the time-honored phrases for so long that she thought them sacred. My remarks, though based directly on the Bible, were scandalous to her. She could not tell the difference between her own inbred prejudices and the commandments of God, probably because she was unfamiliar with the teachings of Scripture and had never bothered to examine her own ideas critically in the light of God's Word.

It was this tendency to make unjust judgments that prompted Jesus to tell His opponents, **"Stop judging by mere appearances, and make a right judgment"** (John 7:24).

When we violate this precept, we are not only guilty of injustice, but we may inflict a great deal of injury.

Few people know that James Adair, for more than 25 years the editor of the award-winning *Power* papers for Scripture Press, once nearly flunked journalism. As a junior in high school, he earned a C in journalism on his first report card. Jim decided he would work harder and bring that grade up. His next report card stunned him with an F.

Jim went to the teacher to protest and to explain that he had worked hard to improve his grade. The teacher misinterpreted his appeal as insolence. "You earned a 65," said the teacher, "but now that will be a 60."

Jim kept talking and his grade kept shrinking until the teacher finally gave him a zero.

The teacher must have realized later that he had misjudged a student who needed encouragement, not condemnation, for at semester's end Jim was surprised to get a passing grade—even though he had coasted the rest of the way with a "what's-the-use" feeling. But what if the episode had soured Jim on journalism for good? A whole generation raised on *Power* papers would have been the poorer.

Go slow.

Think.

Don't jump to negative conclusions.

All of this is implied in Jesus' warning to judge righteously. His words plainly reveal that the appearance and the reality are likely to be two different things. Mistrust the appearance and search for the reality is the counsel of Jesus.

But even when we have passed judgment or, more correctly, ascertained that the judgment of God is against a given act or practice, we still must not judge the person.

The most objectionable—truly evil—criticism is that which attacks another's motive.

Some years ago, I served as executive editor of a Sunday School paper which we redesigned to make more appealing to young people. It went from a conventional appearance to using rather garish art, handlettered heads, and an informal style. Some people liked it and some hated it. Some thought it was too "worldly" in appearance, too suggestive of the hippie counterculture. Many people wrote to criticize the paper. Their criticisms were perfectly in order. Even those who asserted that our policy was a wrongful concession to the world were entitled to that view, though we disagreed with them. And we answered in conciliatory fashion.

But some of the criticism was of a different type. Even after we gave a conciliatory reply, some condemned not only our actions but our motives. A passage from one such letter reads: "It is very apparent as to which way you are determined to go. You are trying desperately to excuse yourselves for any action of the past."

I replied: "May I ask how you got the special insight suggested by the second paragraph of your recent letter? When you have assumed the prerogatives of God to look into men's hearts, judge their motives, and decide they are 'trying desperately to excuse' themselves, you are in clear violation of the Scriptures you purport to uphold so faithfully. 'Who art thou that judgest another man's servant? to his own master he standeth or falleth. But why dost thou set at nought thy brother? for we shall all stand before the judgment seat of Christ' (Rom. 14:4, 10, KJV)."

Actions we can see—and condemn. Motives we cannot see. Therefore, when we condemn another's motives we are betraying the fact that we are unjust. We are guilty of nurturing within our hearts an unkind, unloving, critical spirit.

When Jesus warned us not to judge others, He primarily had in mind this unkind, critical spirit. This is apparent from the context: **"For in the same way you judge others, you will be judged, and with the measure you use, it will be measured to you"** (Matt. 7:2). If I judge others *kindly,* that is no threat! If I always give others the benefit of the doubt, not criticizing their actions unless there is solid biblical ground to do so, and even then criticizing only the act and never the intent, I will not be threatened by the prospect of receiving the same kind of judgment! What more could I hope for than such eminently fair treatment?

Jesus expressed a profound truth when He stated in this connection that the treatment we give will be the treatment we get. This principle applies not only to judging people but to all interpersonal relationships. Jesus said, **"Do not judge, and you will not be judged. Do not condemn, and you will not be condemned. Forgive, and you will be forgiven. Give, and it will be given to you. A good measure, pressed down, shaken together and running over, will be poured into your lap. For with the measure you use, it will be measured to you"** (Luke 6:37-38).

A critical, sour person will be criticized and disliked by others, and no one is cheated more often than a cheater. On the other hand, all the world wishes well to a generous man. In a sense, humanity is like a great mirror; it reflects back exactly what you display to it. Frown, and your image in the mirror frowns back; smile, and it smiles. If the world is treating you poorly, here's a hint. Try changing what you are transmitting and see if your reception doesn't improve also.

Impressing People

Resenting people and judging people often displaces loving them. A third major enemy of love is vainglory—trying to impress others, using people to bolster our egos. This distortion is deeply rooted in our natures. So much so that Jesus warned against it in relationship to the areas of life in which man ought to be most sincere—his religious observances. **"Be careful not to do your 'acts of righteousness' before men, to be seen by them. If you do, you will have no reward from your Father in heaven"** (Matt. 6:1).

Jesus then applied this principle to giving to the needy (vv. 2-4), praying (vv. 5-15), and fasting (vv. 16-18).

The Pharisees of Jesus' day were so infected with this vainglory that it marred every facet of their lives. Jesus said, **"Everything they do is done for men to see: They make their phylacteries wide and the tassels of their prayer shawls long; they love the place of honor at banquets and the most important seats in the synagogues; they love to be greeted in the market-places and to have men call them 'Rabbi' "** (Matt. 23:5-7).

Our lives, like those of the Pharisees, are shot through with attempts to impress others. Advertising unabashedly appeals to that motive, urging us to think how impressed our neighbors will be when they see a brand new Chromemobile in our driveway. Or how heads will turn when we wear our new Johnny Tonight suit before admiring onlookers for the first time.

Many conversations between acquaintances are little more than an exercise in who can impress whom the most. Listen to the voices of children at play:

Joe: "My dad had lunch yesterday with the governor!"

Bobby: "So what? *My* dad once shook hands with the president of the United States."

Milford: "Aw, that's nothin'! *My* dad knows Hank Aaron personally!"

Refine that just a bit, and you have a typical adult exchange:

Joan: "Well, of course, it wasn't anything special to my husband Ted, but he was invited to the governor's luncheon; seems he's always going to some important function."

Roberta: "How nice. Has he ever been to the White House? My husband George never had been until last year."

Millie: "Oh, my dears, how wonderful that *your husbands* have been allowed to meet such important public figures. By the way, did you know that my husband is a personal friend of Billy Graham?"

This phenomenon even affects ministers' gatherings. Pastors ask one another about the success of their respective churches and grope in their minds for achievements for which they can be "humbly grateful."

Why do we behave this way?

Why are we so eager to impress?

Is it not that we want to feel within ourselves that we are important, and to have others recognize it too?

In itself the desire to be important is not wrong. But we can seldom establish our importance by announcing it to people. If we do manage to impress them, they are likely to resent us for making them feel small and unimportant. After all, they have a basic psychological need to feel worthwhile and of value just as we do.

The Power of Service

Jesus told us how we could *be* important. *Being* is the principle thing here. "'Most men will proclaim every one his own goodness, but a faithful man who can find?" (Prov. 20:6) If we only make ourselves *seem* important, we will not be satisfied inwardly, knowing we are phonies. Furthermore, we can't fool people all the time. If we don't really amount to much as people, it will come out sooner or later, usually sooner. So, the question is, how can we truly be important?

Jesus said, **"You know that the rulers of the Gentiles lord it over them, and their high officials exercise authority over them. Not so with you. Instead, whoever wants to become great among you must be your servant, and whoever wants to be first must be your slave—just as the Son of man did not come to be served, but to serve, and to give His life a ransom for many"** (Matt. 20:25-28).

These words of Jesus are a major stumbling block to many people. They figure if one has to become a slave to others to be great in God's sight, it's hardly worth it. To them, Jesus is expressing an idealistic, self-sacrificing standard that is way beyond the average man. One would have to be a superhuman saint to live this way.

Actually, quite the contrary is true. Jesus was here expressing a basic principle or law of life governing interpersonal relationships. The principle applies universally, to Christian and non-Christian alike. And it would be true even if there were no God to pin the "Great Person" label on the one who best serves others.

To verify the truth and the practical application of Jesus' words, you have only to observe life as it is around you. Whom do you esteem? And whom do you count of little worth? Do you not esteem most those who contribute most to you or to others? Those you esteem least are those who contribute least, those who are all take and no give, those who are only served and do not serve others.

This principle may be seen in operation all through our society. Yes, even in this fallen, sinful society that is so far from the ideals of God.

Who *are* the giving people in society? Who contributes most to others? Who serves the public welfare best?

Medical doctors serve the tremendously important function of helping us preserve life and health. Society honors them with respect and money.

Ministers serve people's spiritual needs and they are also esteemed members of society, even if they are not always well paid.

Educators serve us by teaching our children, equipping them intellectually and with skills to succeed in life. This is a great service, and where it is actually rendered, teachers are honored.

Laborers serve us by providing goods and services essential or important to us, and the laboring man is a respected member of our society.

Perhaps one of the best examples is the politician. His occupation is even called "public service." If he is true to that noble description, if he really uses his office to serve the public welfare, he is highly esteemed. If he uses the office to serve his own interests, he is resented and despised. It is precisely this—the suspicion that politicians are self-serving—that sometimes threatens to bring the whole profession into disrepute.

Who are the taking people? Who is it that is only served, and does not serve others? The criminal, the welfare recipient, the incapacitated, the insane. Which of these is honored by society today?

Notice that even if failure to serve is through no fault of their own (as with the insane, some of the unemployed, the incapacitated), they are still ranked with those least honored and least respected in society.

One might protest that these should not be considered inferior to anyone else. Exactly. They "should not be," but they are. That is how far removed from pure idealism the principle of *achieve greatness through service* really is. Jesus was not telling us how things should be in an ideal society when He said that whoever wants to become great must serve. He was telling it like it is!

Even if one knows this, however, he can hardly embark on a life of genuine service to others if he is hurting so much himself that he is virtually unmindful of others. That's the beauty of knowing Jesus. He does not just tell us to serve others. He heals us of our crippling attitudes and preoccupations so that we can serve others.

When Jesus sent out the original Twelve to serve a sick and sin-cursed world, He told them, **"Freely you have received, freely give"** (Matt. 10-8). They could give to others because they had received from God. With Jesus, *come* always precedes *go*. We must come to Him for whatever we need before we can go for Him in service.

If you are in no condition to freely give, maybe it's because you are empty, hurting, burdened. **"Come to Me,"** Jesus said, **"and I will give you rest"** (Matt. 11:28).

11

What Did Jesus Say About . . .

MARRIAGE
And DIVORCE?

Marriage is God's crucible. If a man would stay single, he'd save himself a lot of grief.

As terrible as those statements may sound, they accurately, if only partially, reflect Jesus' teaching on the subject.

Since this claim is unconventional if not actually scandalous, the reader can hardly be expected to readily agree. But let's examine the record.

It's interesting that Jesus hardly talked about marriage apart from the associated question of divorce. Of course, divorce is the subject He was asked about. "Some Pharisees came to Him to test Him. They asked, 'Is it lawful for a man to divorce his wife for any and every reason?' " (Matt. 19:3)

The Scripture says that the motive behind their question was to test Jesus. Two schools of thought concerning divorce were dominant in Jesus' day. We might describe one as the "easy divorce" position and the other as the "strict divorce" view. The former argued that the Law permitted a man to divorce his wife at will, for any reason whatever. The latter maintained that only gross sexual infidelity justified divorce. The controversy hinged on the interpretation of a phrase in Deuteronomy: "When a man hath taken a wife, and married her, and it come to pass that she find no favor in his eyes, *because he hath found some uncleanness in her,* then let him write her a bill of divorcement, and give it in her hand, and send her out of his house" (24:1).

"Easy divorce" advocates argued that the man was here constituted as the sole judge of what comprised "some uncleanness" in his wife. Therefore, in effect, he could divorce her at will. "Strict divorce" proponents insisted that "uncleanness" referred specifically to sexual infidelity and that such behavior had to be clearly established before a marriage could be dissolved.

In replying to the question as to which position was right, Jesus reminded His hearers, in effect, that arguing over "easy divorce" versus "strict divorce" could obscure the more basic principle that *no divorce* is in the plan of God.

Jesus pointed back to the original pattern established at Creation. " 'Haven't you read,' He replied, 'that at the beginning the Creator "made them male and female,"' and said, "For this reason a man will leave his father and mother and be united to his wife, and the two will become one flesh"?' " (vv. 4-5; see also Gen. 2:24)

What was the original creative design of God? One man was joined to one woman. This superceded the otherwise closest of human ties (parent-child). The married couple actually became one in the eyes of God. Based on this, Jesus said that divorce ought not to enter into the scene. **"So they are no longer two, but one. Therefore what God has joined together, let man not separate"** (v. 6).

It would be in order here to pause just enough to observe that Jesus' brief description of marriage quickly rules out the kinky distortions that from time to time arise and pretend legitimacy. "Male and female" excludes so-called marriages of homosexuals. "Two will become one" leaves no room for group sex; it doesn't say "two or more." And Jesus certainly excluded trial marriages or casual liaisons which omit lifelong commitment when He said they are no longer two but one, and are never to separate.

Jesus' admonition that divorce has no place in the plan of God went down rather lumpy with the Pharisees. " 'Why then,' they asked, 'did Moses command that a man give his wife a certificate of divorce and send her away?' " (v. 7) One can imagine them hastily hunting up the controversial Deuteronomy passage, cited earlier, to nail Jesus with a proof text in support of their argument.

"Jesus replied, **'Moses permitted you to divorce your wives because your hearts were hard. But it was not this way from the beginning'** " (v. 8). Note the important distinction. The Pharisees asked why Moses *commanded* divorce; Jesus replied that he *permitted* it, not commanded it, and he only permitted it under circumstances of spiritual and moral declension.

Moses' regulations were calculated to curb the worst abuses of divorce as they existed in his day. In the then prevailing social structure women had few rights. Apart from Moses' ordinance, a man might simply put his wife out into the street to become a prey. Moses commanded that she be given a formal bill of divorcement, and he required that she be shown respect and certain considerations (see Deut. 21:14; 22:13-19, 28-29; 24:1-4).

None of this divorce business, however, was in the will and plan of God. If we are going to talk about what's *right,* divorce is excluded. That was Jesus' teaching.

But right is not always done. Some have well pointed out that hearts were probably no harder in Moses' day when divorce was permitted "because your hearts were hard" than they are now. While divorce is an evil, therefore, may it not sometimes be the lesser of the evil alternatives facing a person?

Jesus did seem to teach that divorce might be an option in cases of marital infidelity. **"I tell you that anyone who divorces his wife, *except for marital unfaithfulness*, and marries another woman commits adultery"** (v. 9).

This so-called "except clause" is the subject of controversy among Christians today as the Deuteronomy law was among the Jews. Some explain the clause away entirely and insist there is no legitimate ground for divorce today. Others permit divorce but not remarriage. Still others feel that adultery is grounds for both divorce and remarriage. Some of these also argue there are other such grounds besides adultery, for example, desertion of a Christian by a non-Christian spouse (1 Cor. 7:15).

Often there is such preoccupation with debate over the "except clause" that the rest of Jesus' important teaching on marriage is almost ignored.

In this connection, the disciples' response to Jesus' teaching is fascinating. They said, "If this is the situation between a husband and wife, it is better not to marry" (v. 10). If a man is going to be stuck with one woman for the rest of his life, he'd be better off to stay single than to risk making a bad choice.

You might say that the disciples did not have a very high view of marriage!

On the other hand, you might say that they were realistic. They had probably seen many bad marriages, some perhaps firsthand. If they were to have the option of divorce as an alternative in a matrimonial disaster, it might make sense to take the chance. But if they were stuck for life . . . ?

The same sort of realistic disillusionment with marriage has led people to seek various alternatives to the one-man-one-woman-for-life pattern. It was not from observing happily married parents that many young couples decided in the '60s and '70s to just live together. A no-marriage-now-and-no-divorce-later arrangement seemed to make sense to them. They certainly didn't want to be trapped in a loveless marriage that they could neither endure nor dissolve.

But if the disciples' low-view-of-marriage response was fascinating, Jesus' response was revolutionary. When the disciples said that with divorce ruled out "it is better not to marry," Jesus virtually *agreed!* He replied, **"Not everyone can accept that, but only those to whom it has been given"** (v. 11).

Then Jesus revealed what He meant by **"those to whom it has been given."** He spoke of various kinds of eunuchs. In the strict definition, a eunuch is a castrated male. A servant selected to take care of a harem would be castrated, for obvious reasons. As Jesus used the term, He probably referred to men who had no strong sexual needs, not necessarily those who were literally castrated.

But notice what Jesus said. **"The one who can accept this should accept it"** (v. 12). In other words, if a man can accept the idea that the single state is better, having no necessity sexually for marriage, he should stay single. Or to state it negatively, don't get married unless you have to because of your sex drive.

I can almost hear screams of protest rising from readers' lips. "Marriage is for more than sex." / "Marriage can be a wonderful, mutually fulfilling relationship." / "The single state is unnatural; God even said it is not good for man to be alone."

All of these cries have merit. I think Jesus would agree with them for the most part. Nevertheless, His words still stand and must be reckoned with. What are the facts?

No doubt God's *rule* for man is marriage. Not many men can meet Jesus' qualifications for staying single. That is, most men have sex drives that demand fulfillment. Therefore, note how God boxes men in.

1. He endows them with strong sex drives.
2. He limits fulfillment of the sex drive to marriage.
3. He forbids divorce.

What is the result? Man must have sex, but he may not have it outside marriage. If he marries, he may not divorce his wife, however shrewish she may be or however another woman catches his fancy.

Man is truly in a crucible, and its name is *marriage*.

What conclusions are inferred by Jesus' teaching?

1. The single state should be considered a viable option. Nobody should marry just because it is the socially accepted thing. If God has given a man the exceptional gift of no need for sex, he should seek, as the Apostle Paul did, to use his single state to best advantage in the service of the Lord (see 1 Cor. 7:7-9, 32-35).

2. A man of normal sexual drives should marry for life. His wife will not be perfect. It may take years for them to develop a beautiful relationship, *even if they work at it*. Otherwise, they could be in for a long ordeal of hurting each other while learning nothing. But note, marriage has the potential to refine and develop the character as few other relationships can. And that is the reason for the crucible.

I have been married for more than 25 years to one woman. We have been in the crucible. Today, our marriage is better than it has ever been, though I could not have said that all the way along and we still have our problems. We still exasperate and frustrate one another. We still have to forgive one another . . . and overlook a lot of things that could otherwise build into major conflicts.

We have had rocky times. We have had times when only the fact that we were Christians kept us together. We have had other times when even that might not have kept us together if changes hadn't come. That's what happens in the crucible. Changes come. Needed changes.

I have often been the typically inconsiderate husband. Once at the annual convention of the National Association of Evangelicals meeting in Portland, Oregon, I was to meet the speaker of the morning after his address and take him to lunch. As an editor, I was going to discuss with him the possibility of his writing for Victor Books. The speaker was Stuart Briscoe.

Since my wife was along, she was going to lunch with us, but my attention was very much on Briscoe and very little on my wife. As we went through the door of the auditorium, I let her fall behind. Mr. Briscoe, always the British gentleman, noticed her a split second before I remembered my manners. As he made way for her, I introduced them.

"I thought it must be your wife," he said good-naturedly. "You surely would not have treated any other woman that way!"

It was a blow well struck and a friendly rebuke well received.

Feminine feelings often don't mean much to pragmatic males, but marriage changes a man. He learns to try to meet the needs of his wife instead of being completely self-centered. At least, he'd better if he doesn't want to live with a miserable woman.

Admittedly, this chapter has presented a fragmentary and male-slanted view of matrimony. Remember, it does not purport to be a thorough and balanced treatment of marriage and divorce. It is rather a discussion of *what Jesus said* on the subject. (The same observation also applies to some extent to the other subjects discussed in this book.)

Suffice it to say here that the wife is in the crucible too. Thus, she learns to meet her husbands needs, including the sexual need that probably was one of the major reasons he got married in the first place. At least, she had better learn to meet that need if she expects the marriage to survive in any positive manner.

Marriage? It's wonderful. Many are the joys shared, the days enriched. But it's even better as a crucible of the soul in which God can really do His work.

12

What Did Jesus Say About . . .

LIFE HEREAFTER?

Life is made up of choice and no choice situations. In some areas, we have options; in others, we do not.

We had *no choice about being born*. In other words, we have to live. Oh, of course, we could commit suicide, but we would still have lived. With absolutely no voluntary participation on our part, we came into being.

However, we have a choice *how* we live. We can life selfishly or unselfishly. We can live timidly or boldly. We can live on an animal plane, gratifying our physical desires only, or we can rise to things of the spirit also. We can live honestly or live in a world of pretense and illusion.

We have some choice not only *how* but *how long* we live. We can, as already suggested, commit suicide. Apart from killing ourselves outright, we can also commit a subtle form of suicide by giving ourselves over to destructive practices, attitudes, and habits. Or we can prolong our lives by eating, resting, and exercising properly and by maintaining a merry heart.

So we can't choose whether to live, but we can choose, to some degree, the quality of our lives.

We also have *no choice but to live in relationship to others*. Oh, of course, we could become hermits, but that would not change the fact that we are related to others, though now that relationship would be one of rejection and neglect.

Actually, it is so difficult as to be practically impossible for anyone, even a hermit, to live without others. Would such a man produce everything he uses from shoes to medicines to all his food and shelter? Would he read nothing, never listen to the radio or watch TV, make all his own tools?

We must live with others, but we can choose *how* we live with others. We can live in suspicion and in hostile competition, or we can have a supportive and cooperative attitude. We can try to always take (or always give), or we can recognize we need to both give and take. We can view people as interruptions to life or as the chief stuff of which life is made.

We have no choice but to live with others, but we do have a choice how we live with them.

We have *no choice but to die,* but we can choose how we die, whether with composure and confidence or with regret and despair.

We have *no choice but to live again,* but we can choose what our life hereafter will be like.

It is at this point—concerning life hereafter—that people often confuse necessity and choice. Some people plainly tell us they don't want to live forever. They believe that death will end all for them, and they don't care to look at options for any kind of a life hereafter.

The trouble is, man has no choice but to live forever. Like being born, living with others, and dying, the future existence is not optional. Not according to Jesus.

"Do not be amazed at this, for a time is coming when all who are in their graves will hear His voice and come out—those who have done good will rise up to live, and those who have done evil will rise to be condemned" (John 5:28-29).

"No way is the body going to come out of this grave," agreed the workmen as they surveyed a tomb they had just sealed. The woman buried there had been a bitter antagonist of the Christian faith. She had left instructions to seal her tomb with steel-reinforced concrete. On it were engraved the words "DEAD FOREVER." Below was inscribed: "Marvel not at this: for the hour is never coming when the person in this grave will hear His or any other voice. She will never come forth, either to a resurrection of life or a resurrection of damnation."

One year later, from a tiny crack in the concrete, there grew a slender stem. Within a few years the grave was literally split wide open by the trunk of the tree that had grown from that insignificant plant. The power of life had burst the bands of steel and concrete as if to symbolize the futility of the woman's efforts. She had opted for a choice that was not hers to make.

What happens after our resurrection is optional; our resurrection itself is not.

In Jesus' day, there were people who did not believe in a resurrection, just as there are now. "Some of the Sadducees, who say there is no resurrection, came to Jesus with a question" (Luke 20:27). Their hypothetical case was designed to embarrass Jesus with regard to His teaching about resurrection and to show how complicated it would be to resurrect everybody.

The Sadducees' question involved the Levitical law which provided for a man whose brother died childless to marry the widow. The first son of such a union would be considered the child of the dead brother. That way his name and family line would be continued. Subsequent children would belong to the second, the surviving husband, so that he wouldn't be giving up his own line of succession. It was a voluntary arrangement, but was considered the virtuous thing to do.

Now, said the Sadducees, suppose this should happen to seven brothers. They all, in turn, are married to the same woman. It's going to get pretty complicated hereafter when everyone is raised!

First, Jesus answered the specific question. Such a situation would raise no problems whatever in the next life because marriage will no longer be in effect (Luke 20:34-35). Jesus said they **"will neither marry nor be given in marriage."** The question of the Sadducees did not concern *contracting new marriages* in the hereafter but the effect of marriages already established here. Unless Jesus meant there would be *no marriage relationship* in heaven, His answer was not responsive to their question. And His adversaries would no doubt have pointed that out!

Next, Jesus went beyond the specific question of the Sadducees to deal with their real argument: that there is no resurrection. He said, **"But in the account of the bush, even Moses showed that the dead rise, for he calls the Lord 'the God of Abraham, and the God of Isaac, and the God of Jacob.' He is not the God of the dead, but of the living, for to Him all are alive"** (Luke 20:37-38).

Note the remarkable argument here:

1. **"Even Moses showed that the dead rise."** Jesus cited Moses because the Sadducees accepted only the first five books of

the Bible as authoritative Scripture, and those books were written by Moses. In other words, if Jesus showed them that even Moses taught the resurrection, they would be forced to accept the doctrine to be consistent with their claimed allegiance to Moses.

2. **"To Him all are alive."** When God appeared to Moses in the phenomenon of a burning bush that was not consumed, He was called the God of Abraham, Isaac, and Jacob. Those three patriarchs had died several hundred years before Moses was born. Yet, since God is not the God of the dead but of the living, the implication is that those long dead patriarchs were alive in Moses' day, though their bodies had decayed in the tomb.

It would seem that this argument of Jesus better proves the immortality of the soul than the resurrection of the body. The day of resurrection was yet future even when Jesus spoke these words, centuries after Moses ("a time is *coming* . . ." John 5:28). The patriarchs were indeed alive unto God in Moses' day, for "to Him all are alive," but they were *not yet resurrected.*

It would be easy to get into philosophic waters over our heads at this point. When Jesus says that to God "all are alive," does that include people not yet born as well as those who have died?

Why not? Being finite, we are cooped up in a time frame. God lives in eternity. We speak of past, present, and future, and find the terms useful. But all tenses are the same to God. What is, *is.* Literally, "to Him all are alive."

But this is beyond us. We shake our heads in puzzlement and move on.

The question remains, how does the Moses record show more than immortality at best? How does it show resurrection?

Here we need to consider the question, *what is a man?* When God said, "I am the God of Abraham," how are we to conceive of Abraham? A whole man is a person *in a body.* When God made man, He formed him from the dust of the earth—a body. Any existence a man may have apart from his body is not as the complete man God intended him to be from the beginning. A man by definition includes a body. This is normative man. So whatever the illusions of time may say about a person being dead or alive, "to Him all are alive," and that includes physical life. There has to be a resurrection because the normative and perpetual state of man involves physical life! This is a bit hard to grasp, but it seems to be what Jesus had in mind.

Heaven or Hell—Real Places?

Some people have wondered whether heaven and hell should be thought of as literal places. The various descriptions of hell—as a lake of fire, as outer darkness, as a garbage dump—have suggested to some minds that these are all figures of something very bad but not necessarily literal descriptions of a place.

Heaven, some tell us, is as mythical as Buss Island. Supposedly discovered by famed explorer Martin Frobisher in 1578, Buss Island was given to Hudson's Bay Company by royal charter in 1675. Though the island continued to appear on charts for nearly three centuries, no one could ever find it (*The Prairie Overcomer,* September 1974, Three Hills, Alberta).

However, the fact that everyone is to receive a real body necessitates that everyone will be in a literal place, whether the biblical descriptions of those places are figurative or not. A body has to be somewhere.

What Is Heaven Like?

The Bible gives only sketchy information about heaven. The word *heaven* itself is very imprecise. The same Greek word is used for the atmosphere, for the celestial heavens, and for the abode of God and of the righteous. Heaven is the sky, so far as the word itself is concerned.

Yuri Gagarin, the Russian cosmonaut, announced on his return from space that he had seen no evidence of God up there. Bishop John A. T. Robinson, who wrote *Honest to God,* stated that our modern scientific understanding rules out a God up in heaven because there is no such thing as an absolute "up." Since the world is round, "up" to the man in China is the opposite direction from "up" to a man in the United States.

The average Christian is not very impressed by the reasoning of either the atheistic Communist or the doubting bishop. What an incredibly anthropomorphic concept of God is required to quibble about the place of His residence, as these two have. God is not a man, and, as Solomon was wise enough to know more than 25 centuries before Gagarin and Robinson appeared on the scene, "Behold, heaven and the heaven of heavens cannot contain Thee" (2 Chron. 6:18).

Nevertheless, the sky is a pretty big place, to understate the facts, and Gagarin would have had to travel a lot farther and faster than he did to justify any declaration that God is not in residence out there.

However, Jesus did not concern Himself with telling us much about the geographical location or even the direction of heaven. He had a lot more to say about its conditions.

"Great is your reward in heaven," He said concerning those who suffer on earth for righteousness' sake (Luke 6:23). Whatever and wherever heaven is, it's a place where God's people can be immensely rewarded. They will have personal identity and self-consciousness to receive the benefit (it is *"your* reward"), and the benefit will be lavishly bestowed (*"great* is your reward").

"I am going there to prepare a place for you," Jesus said (John 14:2). Jesus has now been in heaven nearly 2,000 years carrying on this work of preparing us a place. Judging by what He did in six days at the time of earth's creation, that must be some place He's preparing now!

Of course, it is not the grandeur or glory of the place that is most special about heaven. It is the company. **"If I go and prepare a place for you, I will come back and take you to be with Me that you also may be where I am"** (John 14:3).

When Jesus was here on earth, only three of His closest disciples were privileged to see Him transfigured on the mountain. "His face shone like the sun, and His clothes became as white as the light" (Matt. 17:2). They never got over it.

John later wrote, "We have seen His glory, the glory of the one and only Son, who came from the Father, full of grace and truth" (John 1:14).

Peter wrote, "We were eyewitnesses of His majesty. For He received honor and glory from God the Father when the voice came to Him from the Majestic Glory, saying, 'This is My Son, whom I love; with Him I am well-pleased.' We ourselves heard this voice that came from heaven when we were with Him on the sacred mountain" (2 Peter 1:16-18).

But the privilege then afforded only to Peter, James, and John will belong to all Christians in the hereafter. Jesus specifically prayed that it might be so, **"Father, I want those You have given Me to be with Me where I am, and to *see My glory*, the glory You have given Me because You loved Me before the creation of the world"** (John 17:24).

To see the glory of Christ will be the highlight of eternity!

Yet there is more.

Christians are not going to be nameless, faceless spectators in the heavenly courts. Jesus said, **"I tell you, whoever acknowledges Me before men, the Son of Man will also acknowledge him before the angels of God"** (Luke 12:8).

The glorified Christ, whom to see is an amazing privilege, will acknowledge us, will introduce us, if you please, at the court of heaven. Jude exulted in this and spoke of it in the benediction of his brief letter. "To Him who is able to keep you from falling and to present you before His glorious presence without fault and with great joy" (Jude 24).

Jesus is not planning to sneak us in through the back door of heaven. He intends to present us there formally, and He is going to do it "with great joy!" How wonderful, when you consider that we don't deserve to enter the place at all!

When I began seriously dating red-haired Marjorie Iverson, who is now my wife, my mother chided me one day for having never brought her home to meet the family. "Who are you ashamed of," she asked, "her or us?"

I assured her it was neither. Rather, it was only an example of my typical desire for privacy. I guess I figured she was somehow less my special possession if I shared her with the family.

But Jesus is going to delight to share us with the rest of heaven's family. He is not ashamed of us, though He well might be if all our embarrassing sins were to be revealed. But the salvation of Christ is fully adequate. Our sins are gone. He can and will present us in glory with His total approval. What a triumphant moment for Him and for us!

What Is Hell Like?

One shrinks from even contemplating hell. The glories of heaven are so pleasant. Who wants to think about an alternative?

But that's precisely the point. Heaven is so desirable that hell would be a tragedy if it meant nothing more than missing heaven. However, Jesus taught that hell's reality will be far more grim than that. How, specifically, did He describe the destiny of the lost?

A place of fire. **"This is how it will be at the end of the age. The angels will come and separate the wicked from the righteous and throw them into the fiery furnace, where there will be weeping and grinding of teeth"** (Matt. 13:49-50).

A place of darkness. **"Then the king told the attendants 'Tie him hand and foot, and throw him outside, into the darkness, where there will be weeping and grinding of teeth"** (Matt. 22:13).

A loathsome place. **"If your hand causes you to sin, cut it off. It is better for you to enter life maimed than with two hands to go into hell, where the fire never goes out. And if your foot causes you to sin, cut it off. It is better for you to enter life crippled, than to have two feet and be thrown into hell. And if your eye causes you to sin, pluck it out. It is better for you to enter the kingdom of God with one eye, than to have two eyes and be thrown into hell, where 'their worm does not die, and the fire is not put out'"** (Mark 9:43-48).

These sayings of Jesus don't require any comment to be disturbing. They are electric words, fearful words, threatening words.

If the concept of burning in a fiery hell doesn't shake us, it is only because we are numbed to it by overfamiliarity.

While the word pictures Jesus gave of hell need no reinforcing, they could stand a little explanation . . . and a great deal of reflection.

Some have delighted to point out that the word translated *hell* in these passages is the Greek *gehenna,* which refers to the Valley of Hinnom. They ask whether we are really to believe that the lost of all nations and ages are going to be cast into that particular valley in Palestine. Their object, of course, is to deny the existence of a literal hell.

No doubt Jesus did have the garbage dump of Jerusalem, the Valley of Hinnom, in the back of His mind as He spoke. And no doubt we are to understand His words somewhat figuratively. To know that *gehenna* was a garbage dump enlightens us as to why Jesus described it as a place where the worm never dies and the fire never goes out. Carcasses of dead animals, along with every other kind of refuse, were thrown on the garbage dump and burned. The perpetual burning, the acrid smoke, the stench of decaying flesh, the carcasses crawling with maggots combine to form as repulsive a picture as one can imagine.

What must hell be like if Jesus chose to use such a description in attempting to convey its horrors to us?

Jesus seems to have summoned the most fearful images He

could to represent hell. The garbage dump is one of the worst. However, the dread terror of darkness is something almost everyone has experienced. Jesus warns against being cast into outer darkness.

The fear of falling is also basic to human experience, being one of the earliest fears of infants. "Cast into outer darkness" suggests hurtling nightmarishly through the blackness of space.

In addition to using such fearful descriptions, Jesus plainly says that one should take any measure necessary, no matter how extreme, to escape hell. If it requires cutting off one's own hand or foot, or plucking out one's eye, one should do it!

Of course, maiming ourselves will not keep us out of hell. Even if we have used our hands to sin, cutting them off won't prevent our sinning, as the example of Mika (see chap. 2) demonstrates. Sin doesn't originate in the various members of the body but in the heart.

But Jesus is here emphasizing the tremendous stakes for which we play in life. Hell is to be avoided at all costs. Any habit, any personal alliance, any job or occupation should be sacrificed if it endangers one's soul.

The things people choose to keep, rather than sacrificing in order to save their souls from hell, are ridiculous. The rich young ruler chose to keep his wealth rather than save his soul (Matt. 19:16-22). A salesman told me he'd have to quit his job to become a Christian, because, while his product was good and his sales pitch mostly true, it was the 2% lies he told that made the sales. He chose his job rather than Christ.

A young woman would not become a Christian when her husband did because she didn't want to give up dancing! What a paltry thing for which to lose one's soul!

For what trifles people go to hell!

Again, cutting off one's job or dancing or anything else will not in itself keep one from hell. But if holding onto these things, or anything else *whether innocent or evil,* keeps one from receiving Christ as Saviour, then these things do have the effect of condemning one to hell.

Jesus suggested that one should take not only radical action (cut off what offends) but vigorous action. **"If your hand or your foot causes you to sin, cut it off and *throw it away"*** (Matt. 18:8). Much as one might throw a sputtering, short-fused stick of dynamite as far and as fast as his strength permits, one should cast away anything that might condemn him to hell.

How to Have a Happy Hereafter

So far we have said that man has no choice about experiencing an afterlife. His choice is whether it will be a delight to enjoy or an ordeal to endure. And those are *extreme* alternatives. That is, heaven is better, hell worse, than we can possibly describe.

What decides our fate?

The answer to that question is both simple and complex. The application of the answer is both easy and difficult.

Simple and Complex

Jesus said, **"Enter through the narrow gate. For wide is the gate and broad is the road that leads to destruction, and many enter through it. But small is the gate and narrow the road that leads to life, and only a few find it"** (Matt. 7:13-14).

The familiar King James Version renders verse 14: "Strait is the gate, and narrow is the way, which leadeth unto life." From this has come the expression, "Keep on the straight and narrow." This, in turn, has given many people the impression that Christianity is narrow-minded and straight-laced, that it is an austere, extremely difficult, rigorous religion.

This is not what Jesus meant. If it were, He could not have said shortly afterward, **"Come to Me, all you who are weary and burdened, and I will give you rest. Take My yoke upon you and learn from Me, for I am gentle and humble in heart, and you will find rest for your souls. For My yoke is easy and My burden is light"** (Matt. 11:28-30).

What *did* Jesus mean then? Simply that there is a broad way, easy to find and filled with great throngs, that leads to hell. But the way to heaven is not so easy to find and it is not so well-travelled.

Actually, any road you care to blunder down can take you to hell. You can get there via atheism or agnosticism or man-made religions of various stripes or preoccupation with worldly desires or simple indifference to God. But you cannot get to heaven via many routes. Jesus said, **"I am the way—and the truth and the life. No one comes to the Father except through Me"**

(John 14:6). The way is so narrow as to be singular: it is by Jesus alone.

The way to heaven is also narrow in that you must enter it individually. Heaven doesn't issue any group insurance policies, nor does it have group entry fees. You must make personal application to God for forgiveness of your sins and you must personally acknowledge Jesus Christ as your Lord and Saviour.

It is the first of these singularities—entry is by Jesus alone—that the Lord no doubt had in mind when He spoke of the narrow way, for He immediately proceeded to warn against plausible false prophets. **"They come to you in sheep's clothing, but inwardly they are ferocious wolves"** (Matt. 7:15). Jesus went on to say we could recognize them by their evil fruit. However, since He had already told us they masquerade in sheep's clothing, He did not mean they were immediately recognizable as false on the basis of their *appearance.*

It's too bad that not all people who speak in the name of religion can be trusted. We'd like to think they could be. Jesus clearly warns us they cannot. We must judge them by their fruit.

This gets complicated. Most religions in the world, including the fringe cults of Christianity and the non-Christian religions such as Judaism, Islam, and Hinduism, teach good morals. Many of the adherents of these religions live "good" lives. If these good lives are the "fruit," all these religions would seem to be vindicated. But that contradicts what Jesus said about the way to life being narrow, singular.

Perhaps we need to examine the passage more closely. Jesus is talking about the fruit of false and true prophets. May I suggest that a prophet's fruit is *his prophecy.* And the absolute test of whether a prophet is true or false is whether his prophecy is good or bad. And how do we decide that? "To the Law and to the Testimony: if they speak not according to this Word, it is because there is no light in them" (Isa. 8:20).

In other words, we must measure religious teachers by how their teachings square with those of God's Word. And we must do so remembering that their personal attractive qualities or their claims to base everything on the Bible may be no more than the sheep's clothing Jesus warned about.

How does all this relate to our fate in the hereafter? By revealing both the simplicity and complexity of the way to heaven. It's simple: Jesus Christ is the only Way to God. But it's complex too, because there are many false prophets around to mislead us about Him and the nature of saving faith. We have to reject their error and embrace the Scripture's truth. Otherwise our "Jesus" may not be the One who is the way to God at all but a false "Jesus" of man's own devising.

Easy and Difficult

Even when we know who Jesus really is, we still can miss heaven. We can call Him "Lord, Lord," which is His true identity, without ever truly making Him *our Lord,* the One whom we obey. Not he who *says* "Lord" but he who *lives* "Lord," that is *obeys* Christ, will enter the kingdom of heaven (see Matt. 7:21).

Jesus said it was not only possible to call Him Lord without obeying Him and being saved, but that this would be the case with "many" (v. 22).

The life that will culminate in heaven hereafter is the one marked by a personal relationship with Jesus Christ on earth now. The only personal relationship possible between the Lord Jesus Christ and us humans is one which includes our obedience and His Lordship, for that is the very nature of the divine-human relationship. We are not functioning as *His people* unless we obey. He is not our acknowledged *Lord* unless He is obeyed.

Those whose "faith" in Christ has not produced a life marked by obedience to Him will one day hear Him say to them, **"I never knew you. Away from Me, you evildoers!"** (v. 23) Thus He will strip away their claims, which have at all times been false, never having been based on submission to His lordship.

Every day as we go along, we are building a life (Matt. 7:24-27). We are either building it on Christ and His teachings or we are building it apart from Christ and His teachings. The life built without Christ, however well-built, with whatever pains, and at however great a cost, will end in collapse. The life built upon Christ may be called upon to endure many storms, but it will stand.

You have no choice about living hereafter. You still have a choice, now, of what kind of hereafter it will be.

13
What Did Jesus Say About . . .
HIS RETURN?

A gentle old man was visiting his son's family and was invited to attend church services with them. In the adult Bible class, a discussion arose concerning some details of Christ's second coming. It soon became apparent that a difference of opinion existed, particularly between two outspoken members of the class. These two began defending their ideas in stronger and stronger terms until they were practically fighting, each belittling the other's views.

Later, the man's son said, "Dad, you didn't say anything. You are a student of the Scriptures. Which man was right?"

"Neither," said the father. "Oh, one of them may have been closer to the right views, but you didn't ask which *views* were right but which *man* was right."

The interpretation of prophecy is debatable, but when a person is unloving and unkind, there is *no question about that being wrong*. We too often forget that it is more important for the heart to be right than the head.

No area of our examination into the sayings of Jesus is so likely to raise objections from those who have a different interpretation as the one to which we now come. Is it possible to approach the subject of Christ's second coming with an open mind, laying aside all presuppositions associated with various eschatological systems, and find out what Jesus said and meant? Let's at least try it. And if we disagree, let's do so in love.

One thing is clear. Jesus has a return on His schedule. He referred to it frequently. For example, **"There are many rooms**

in My Father's house; otherwise, I would have told you. I
am going there to prepare a place for you. And if I go and
prepare a place for you, *I will come back* and take you to be
with Me that you also may be where I am" (John 14:2-3).

Does It Mean Death?

"I will come back," seems clear enough. Yet some think Jesus was
speaking here of the believer's death. The passage does talk about
our going to be with Him, not His coming to stay with us. The
death of a Christian may be beautifully described as the Lord
Jesus coming for us, some suggest.

When Stephen was stoned to death, he saw Jesus standing at
the right hand of God (Acts 7:55). Scripture usually pictures the
Son as *seated* at the Father's right hand. Some speculate that Jesus
was rising to come for Stephen. Others say, however, that He only
rose to receive the first martyr of the Church, as the latter was
about to enter heaven.

Nowhere does Scripture clearly say that death involves Jesus'
coming for us. Jesus' own statement that the Apostle John *might*
remain alive until His coming (John 21:22) wouldn't make sense
if His "coming" referred to death. Obviously John would live
until he died!

Passages such as 1 Thessalonians 4:14-17 eliminate the possibility that the Lord's coming is only a euphemism for death. There
we read both about believers who die before His return and those
who are alive at His return. No believer *could* die before His "return" if the two were synonomous (see also 1 Cor. 15:51-52).

Does It Mean Pentecost?

Some have suggested that when Jesus spoke of His return, He
was really referring to His coming back in the person of the Holy
Spirit on the Day of Pentecost. That "coming of Christ" began
His glorious kingdom here on earth, they say.

Those who take this position point to the occasions when Jesus
said that His return was imminent. He told the disciples, for example, **"I tell you the truth, some who are standing here will
not taste death before they see the Son of man coming in
His kingdom"** (Matt. 16:28). Since all of the original disciples
have died long since, this "coming in His kingdom" of which
Jesus spoke cannot be a literal advent still future. Some say that

He meant only that the disciples would see Him transfigured (have a foreglimpse of His kingdom glory), as described in the next chapter, Matthew 17. Others insist, however, that He was talking about His return in the Person of the Holy Spirit at Pentecost.

Is it legitimate to call the Holy Spirit's coming a return of Christ? Or is that an inadmissible confusing of the distinct persons of the Godhead?

Apparently, it is biblical to speak of the Holy Spirit's coming as a return of Christ, for Jesus did so! Preparing His disciples for His departure, He assured them, **"I will not leave you as orphans; I will come to you"** (John 14:18). The immediate context shows that Jesus was referring to the coming of the Holy Spirit when He spoke those words. Later in the same conversation, Jesus said that both He and the Father would come to "make Our home with" the believer (v. 23). Obviously, He meant that They would come in the Person of the Holy Spirit.

The question remaining is whether *all* of the references to Christ's return can be satisfied by applying them to Pentecost and the establishment of the Church. Such an application certainly solves the problem of why Jesus indicated His return would be almost immediate. However, it does not explain why He also taught that His return would *not* be immediate.

"He went on to tell them a parable, because He was near Jerusalem and the people thought that the kingdom of God was going to appear at once" (Luke 19:11). The corrective parable that follows describes a prince who goes to a distant country and is gone long enough for his servants to demonstrate how well they can administer his affairs and invest his money during his absence.

One could explain the going into a distant country to receive a kingdom as representing Christ's ascension into heaven and exaltation to the Father's right hand. Pentecost could then represent His return. But the 10 days between His ascension and Pentecost could hardly be parallel to the period during which the servants invested or failed to invest their master's resources. The time is much too short. The parallel breaks down even further when one considers that Jesus specifically told the disciples to tarry in Jerusalem, that is, to delay their active ministry until after Pentecost. Such a procedure on their part resembles the unfaithful servant more than it does the faithful servants of the parable (Luke 19:20).

A Literal Return Assured

Even if many of the prophecies of Jesus' "return" may be applied to other events, the Bible makes it plain that He is actually going to come again in the flesh, visibly and terrestrially. That becomes clear beyond all misunderstanding when we read Acts 1:9-11. "After He said this, He was taken up before their very eyes, and a cloud hid Him from their sight. They were looking intently up into the sky as He was going, when suddenly two men dressed in white stood beside them. 'Men of Galilee,' they said, 'why do you stand here looking into the sky? This same Jesus, who has been taken from you into heaven, will come back in the same way you have seen Him go into heaven.' "

The "same Jesus" is coming back, and He is coming back "the same way" He left. Language could hardly be clearer.

The Olivet Discourse

When will Christ return? What will be the signs of His coming, and of the end of the age? Those are precisely the questions the disciples asked Jesus on one occasion (see Matt. 24:3).

However, the disciples asked their questions in the context of a then-standing temple (vv. 1-2). Jesus had foretold the utter destruction of that temple, and the disciples seem to have assumed that that cataclysmic event would coincide with the end of the age and the Lord's return. Their assumption was far wide of the mark, for the temple was destroyed in A.D. 70, and we are still awaiting the end of the age and the Lord's return some 19 centuries later.

Many people have tried to apply all of the Olivet Discourse to end-time events. They chronicle wars, famines, pestilences, and earthquakes in various places (vv. 6-7) and report that the increase of these plagues signals that the last times are surely upon us. This they do despite Jesus' statement that **"such things must happen, but the end is still to come."** They argue that the statement, **"All these are the beginning of sorrows"** (v. 8, KJV), ought to be translated as our basic text for this book does: **"All these are the beginning of *birth pains*."** How long is it after a woman goes into labor before her child is born? they ask. And they insist, when we see these "birth pain" plagues greatly increase, Christ is about to return.

Still, many remain unconvinced that wars, famines, pestilences, and earthquakes in the news today are prophetically significant.

Communications are so vastly improved that we know about these things much more than we used to, they say. If such disasters were signs of Christ's near return, He would have been back long ago, for the world has always had an abundance of them.

Since the questions of the disciples that gave rise to the Olivet Discourse concerned both the destruction of the temple and the Lord's return (events separated by centuries), some have, sensibly enough, tried to figure out which part of the discourse relates to which.

Some have assigned all of verses 4-13 to that period, now long past, leading up to the destruction of the temple. To them the "end" mentioned in verse 13 (**"But he who stands firm to the end will be saved"**) is the end of the Jewish nation and temple worship. They point out as a matter of historical fact that the Christians who were faithful to the end literally saved their lives. They escaped in time to the Judean hills because they knew the siege of Jerusalem could only end in the city's destruction, as Jesus had warned. Unfaithful Christians perished with the unbelieving Jews when Jerusalem fell. (This explanation of being saved by enduring to the end is especially appealing to Calvinists!)

Others, noting that Jesus does not clearly distinguish which part of His answer relates to which of the disciples' questions, feel that the whole discourse applies to both "ends" (the destruction of the temple in A.D. 70 and the return of Christ in A.D. *??*).

The two epochs will be so similar, they say, that the same prophecies may be applied to both. The destruction of the temple with the attendant sorrows and judgments was a foreshadowing of the events surrounding the Lord's return.

Mission enthusiasts have thought to hasten the return of Christ by reaching the whole world with the Gospel, because Jesus said this would happen before the end (v. 14). Or they have heralded the advent of globe-circling Gospel radio broadcasts as a fulfillment of this prophecy and a sure sign of the Lord's imminent return.

Others deny any prophetic significance to such missionary endeavors; they claim the Gospel was preached in all the world during the very first century, and they cite Scriptures to support their claim (Col. 1:5-6; Acts 8:4).

Since Israel regained control of Mt. Moriah in the Six Day War of 1967, a great deal of speculation has surfaced concerning the possible rebuilding of the temple. Jesus said the key signal for the beginning of "great distress" unequalled in the history of the world (v. 21) would be the desecration of the holy place (v. 15). Obviously, the temple must be rebuilt before it can be desecrated.

Again, however, the prophecy is subject to various interpretations. Antiochus Epiphanes is said to have fulfilled Daniel's prophecy when he desecrated the temple in the second century B.C. by erecting images there and offering swine's flesh on the altar. Though this could be a fulfillment of Daniel's prophecy, it could hardly be *the* fulfillment, because Jesus said that was yet future in His day.

Many students of the Scriptures believe that the desecration of a new Jewish temple will be the work of Antichrist himself. The Apostle Paul wrote, "Don't let anyone deceive you in any way, for that day will not come until the rebellion occurs and the man of lawlessness is revealed, the man doomed to destruction. He opposes and exalts himself over everything that is called God or is worshiped, and even *sets himself up in God's temple,* proclaiming himself to be God" (2 Thes. 2:3-4). Possibly it will be Antichrist's act of temple desecration that will finally reveal his true identity. (Some believe this same situation is in view in Rev. 13:14-15.)

When Will Christ Come?

One of the most controversial segments of Jesus' Olivet Discourse relates to the "time slot" passage. **"Now learn this lesson from the fig tree: As soon as its twigs get tender and its leaves come out, you know that summer is near. Even so, when you see all these things, you know that it is near, right at the door. I tell you the truth, this generation will certainly not pass away until all these things have happened"** (Matt. 24:32-34).

Some have confidently announced that our own generation must see the consummation of biblical prophecy and the return of the Lord. Why? Because the fig tree (the nation of Israel) is budding, and Jesus said the generation that witnessed Israel's restoration would not pass "until all these things have happened." On this basis, some have set 40 years or so as the longest Christ's return could yet be delayed.

The word translated *generation,* however, can refer to a whole race of people. Some believe Jesus was promising that the Jewish race will not perish from the earth, despite history's Hitlers and the end time's Antichrist, but will live to see history consummated in the return of Christ.

Nevertheless, regardless of the meaning of *generation* here, Jesus said **"when you see all these things, you know that it is near, right at the door"** (v. 33). Now the question becomes, see all *what* things? All the things foretold in the entire discourse? Or only the things relating to Israel showing new signs of life? If we can't be sure His coming is near until all the things foretold in the discourse materialize, we are left without clear mileposts at this juncture in time, for the temple has not yet been rebuilt and desecrated.

Can We Resolve Conflicting Views?

If anything can be said with assurance about prophecies concerning end-time events, it is that they are subject to varying interpretations. At almost every point, the Olivet Discourse gives rise to controversial and diverse viewpoints, of which we have mentioned only a few. Some insist that their own interpretation is clearly best. But others of equal scholarship and Christian dedication offer much different explanations of the same texts.

This diversity may be not only one of the most obvious facts about prophecy but also one of the most significant. A mind uncluttered with any elaborate eschatological system to defend must surely ask *why Jesus couldn't explain things a bit more clearly.*

And as surely as the uncluttered or unprejudiced mind must ask such a question, the reverent mind must answer that He was quite capable of making these matters clear *had He wished to do so.*

After all, Jesus did not have to mingle prophecies about His 20th-century-or-later return with those of the A.D. 70 destruction of Jerusalem. He could have stated to the disciples quite plainly, "You will all die and centuries must pass before My return." Why didn't He?

Meditation on these observations soon suggests that Jesus never intended the prophecies about His return to provide a clear and simple picture of the future such as some prophecy experts have so "helpfully" developed.

It is not the *time* of Christ's coming that is primarily important but the *fact* of His coming, and that is the focus of prophecy. As

C. H. Spurgeon said, "People have a panting to know the future; and certain divines pander to this depraved taste, by prophesying for them, and letting them know what is coming by-and-by. I do not know the future, and I shall not pretend to know. But I do preach this, because I know it, that *Christ will come,* for He says so in a hundred passages" (*Searchlight on Spurgeon,* Eric W. Hayden, Pilgrim, 1973).

Indeed, much of the Olivet Discourse seems to be occupied with telling us by parable, illustration, and in so many words that we cannot know the time of Christ's return.

Mainline Christians have always avoided date setting in regard to Christ's return because of the plain words of Jesus: **"No one knows about that day or hour, not even the angels in heaven, nor the Son, but only the Father"** (v. 36). Jesus immediately followed that statement with an illustration. **"As it was in the days of Noah, so it will be at the coming of the Son of Man. For in the days before the flood, people were eating and drinking, marrying and giving in marriage,** *up to the day* **Noah entered the ark; and** *they knew nothing about what would happen until the flood came* **and took them all away. That is how it will be at the coming of the Son of Man"** (vv. 37-39).

The order of the day for Noah's contemporaries was life as usual. They had no sense of impending doom. Right up to the final day, they were living normal lives, even establishing new families, because they knew not the time.

How often this passage has been misinterpreted! Many have declared this to be a prophecy that society will become as corrupt at the end of our age as it was in Noah's day, and that increased eating (gluttony) and drinking (intoxication) and divorce and remarriage will be signs of Christ's return. If they are correct, it is not because of any shred of evidence in this passage to support that view! It only speaks here of life as usual. Eating, drinking, and marrying are not sinful, and the passage doesn't even mention gluttony, drunkenness, or divorce. And the context is: you can't know the time. How ironic that anyone should use the very example Jesus gave for not knowing the time as a sign by which to know the time!

In a parallel passage (Luke 17:26-29), Jesus cited not only the eating-drinking-marrying of Noah's time but also the buying, selling, planting, and building of Lot's time. Are we to see moral degeneracy and a sign of Christ's return in the buying and selling of goods? Or in construction projects or the planting of crops? Is not pursuing these activities rather a sign of life as usual, evidence that people do not know their time has run out? (Why erect a new building or plant a crop that takes weeks to mature if the world ends tomorrow?)

Jesus followed his statement and illustration concerning the unknown time of His return with repeated declarations that we cannot know (Matt. 24:42, 44; 25:13).

The last word Jesus ever spoke on this earth relating to His return is recorded in Acts 1. What was it? Another admonition that the *time* was privileged information. **"It is not for you to know the times or dates the Father has set by His own authority"** (v. 7). Earlier He had said we could not know the day or hour. Now He broadens this to include "times." Why won't we be content with His "it is not for you to know"?

Ever since Christ left, Christians have expected His soon return. At times they have amassed biblical prophecies to prove the end was at hand. In the past, events have always proved the words of Jesus to be true: *they did not know the times or dates after all,* however sure they were of themselves and however much they were able to convince others.

Some have justified their mania for time-setting with the argument that people need to figure out when Christ is coming so that they can *get ready.* This stands in conflict with the words of Jesus; He said that since we are not going to know the time, we should constantly *be ready* (Matt. 25:44).

Make up your mind to it. You will get no more advance notice than did the people who perished in Noah's day or in Lot's. If you expect to be ready when Christ returns, you can't plan to get ready when the time nears, because you won't know when the time nears. *You may be standing on the brink of eternity right now!*

During the dark early days of World War II, I was traveling as a boy with my family from California to Oregon via the Pacific coast route. Dim-out regulations were in effect all along the coast for fear of Japanese attack. Since we were not permitted to drive after dark, we stopped just before nightfall one evening at a seaside motel. Someone in the family suggested it would be delightful to walk along the beach for a few minutes before retiring. By then night had fallen, and observance of the dim-out requirements made the whole area dark indeed.

Taking a dim flashlight, we crossed the deserted highway and walked down a small stub of road that led to the beach. At the end of the road was the typical barricade. In the exuberance of my youth, I had bounded ahead of the others a bit. Now I clambered over the barricade and was about to hop over the edge to the beach.

"Hold it!" called my older sister. "You don't know how far down that is."

We shined the flashlight into the darkness but its feeble beam showed nothing.

Moments later three military vehicles jerked to a halt on the highway just behind us. Out poured the soldiers, their floodlights and the grim-looking muzzles of their guns pointed directly at us.

"Don't shoot," cried my mother in alarm; "we're not invaders!"

"Ordinarily we shoot first and ask questions later!" the squad leader said gruffly. He dressed us down thoroughly for showing a light along the coast and sent us back to our motel.

The next morning we returned to the scene of our folly, to see in the light of day the place where we had almost been shot. We walked down the stub of a road to the barricade. I didn't hop over it now as I had the night before for just beyond was a sheer cliff dropping 40 feet to jagged rocks below!

Where I had stood with total unconcern the night before, I now did not dare to stand at all. I could only gingerly stretch over the barricade to look at the awesome drop.

Just before Jesus comes, multitudes will stand on the brink of destruction with total unconcern. It will not be because the danger is unreal, but only because it is unseen.

Jesus said, **"So you also must *be ready*, because the Son of man will come at an hour when you do not expect Him"** (Matt. 24:44).

A Last Word

Jesus certainly had important and provocative things to say while He was here on earth. We have examined many of these sayings, hopefully with understanding and profit.

However, Jesus has also spoken to man since His return to heaven. These words of Christ are found in Revelation 2 and 3.

One of these latter sayings has been particularly meaningful to multitudes: **"Here I am! I stand at the door and knock. If anyone hears My voice and opens the door, I will go in and eat with him, and he with Me"** (Rev. 3:20).

Notice that Jesus describes Himself as *here* with us standing at the door, knocking, seeking admission into our lives, to "eat" with us—to share daily intimate fellowship.

What is necessary in order for us to know Christ in this personal way? **"If anyone *hears My voice* and *opens the door*, I will go in."**

Probably you have heard His voice speaking to your innermost being as you have pondered His teachings presented in this book and in the Bible. What remains? To "open the door" to Christ.

Why not pray right now? Say, "Jesus, I open my heart's door to You. Please come in. Forgive my sins and be my personal Saviour and Lord."

Remember, He promises, **"If *anyone* . . . opens the door, I will go in."**

The result: God has given us eternal life, and this life is in His Son. *He who has the Son has life;* he who does not have the Son of God does not have life" (1 John 5:11-12). When Christ enters your life, at your invitation, He brings you eternal life!

Make it definite. Pray as suggested above. Then, sign your name below and date it.

"I have specifically opened the door of my life and invited Christ to come in, believing in His promise of eternal life."

Scripture Index

156